The Luminous Dusk

The Luminous Dusk

FINDING GOD
IN THE DEEP, STILL PLACES

Dale C. Allison Jr.

WILLIAM B. EERDMANS PUBLISHING COMPANY
GRAND RAPIDS, MICHIGAN / CAMBRIDGE, U.K.

Published 2006 by

Wm. B. Eerdmans Publishing Co.

255 Jefferson Ave. S.E., Grand Rapids, Michigan 49503 /

P.O. Box 163, Cambridge CB3 9PU U.K.

www.eerdmans.com

Printed in the United States of America

11 10 09 08 07 06   7 6 5 4 3 2 1

Library of Congress Cataloging-in-Publication Data

Allison, Dale C., Jr.

The luminous dusk / Dale C. Allison Jr.

p.   cm.

ISBN-10: 0-8028-3218-0 / ISBN-13: 978-0-8028-3218-4 (pbk. : alk. paper)

1. God.   2. Spiritual life — Christianity.   I. Title.

BT103.A44 2006

248 — dc22

2006006710

Unless otherwise noted, the Scripture quotations in this publication are from the Revised Standard Version of the Bible, copyrighted 1946, 1952 © 1971, 1973 by the Division of Christian Education of the National Council of Churches of Christ in the U.S.A., and used by permission.

Contents

Preface

⌣‿ʌʌ‿⌣

The motes of the air, although always around us, rarely float into view. This is because, without bright sunlight and just the right angle of vision, the dancing specks remain invisible.

In like fashion, I think of this book as a modest light upon some current conditions most of us seldom consider — the growing obscuration of the night sky, for example, and the increasing quantity of artificial images witnessed over the course of a lifetime. The difference is that, whereas the impact of motes is without noticeable effect, the circumstances I shall examine are not.

My presupposition is that human nature is like wet clay on the potter's wheel: the stuff can be shaped into many different forms. We are not, however, inert lumps but rather conscious animals with the gift of freedom. And so the simile is a paradox. The pot is also the potter: we are in our own hands. As it says in the *Dhammapada,* "Well-makers lead the water wherever they like; fletchers bend the arrow; carpenters bend a log of wood; wise people fashion themselves." We may be products of our environment, but we help make the environment. This is why we all need wisdom, and enough imagination to become fully conscious of what we are doing.

Quite a few friends have critically commented upon one or more of the chapters in this volume, and I gratefully acknowledge them here: my wife, Kristine, the late D. Clifford Allison Sr., Kathy Anderson, Paul Boaz, John Burgess, David Cullen, the late W. D. Davies, Harold Fickett, Richard Foster, A. G. Harmon, Jeanine Hathaway, Craig Hinkson, Joel Marcus, the late Jim Naylor, Michael Neth, David Owens, Virginia Stem Owens, Bruce Parmenter, Essie Sappenfield, Russell Smoker, Chris Tachick, Richard Wilkinson, Greg Wolfe, and Suzanne Wolfe.

The introductory chapter grows out of a lecture for the 1994 Fred L. Parrish Colloquium, sponsored by Robert Linder and the History Department of Kansas State University. I am indebted to the lively discussion that followed my presentation. Chapter 1 originally appeared in the Spring 1993 issue of *Image: A Journal of Religion and the Arts* (pp. 85-97), and is reprinted with permission. Chapter 3 revises material that I first used in the New College Lectures delivered at Friends University in 1989. Slightly different versions of Chapter 4 have appeared in *Pulpit Digest* 80/3 (1999), pp. 21-26; in *Panorama* 41/2 (2001), pp. 3-5; and in *Forum: The Quarterly Journal of the Armenian Evangelical Union of North America* 22/4 (December 2001), pp. 15-16. Chapter 7 is a revision of my inaugural lecture for the Errett M. Grable chair in New Testament Exegesis and Early Christianity, Pittsburgh Theological Seminary, given in May of 2000. Earlier editions of the introduction, chapters 1 through 3, and chapters 5 and 6 appeared in *The Silence of Angels* (Trinity Press International, 1994), which is now out of print.

I am pleased to dedicate this book to my lifelong friend, Robert Harrington. He will, despite his very different view of things, find much of himself in it. We met before kindergarten, and, after the vicissitudes of life have finished with us, one of us will no doubt bury the other.

INTRODUCTION

The World around Us

The whole world is inexhaustible by the collective knowledge of all the aeons from the time of creation. All the wise men of all these centuries have not been able to understand fully and precisely a small fragment of this creation. Truly, then, this creation is an ocean that drowns every mind! This is one miracle that leaves every tongue speechless.

Nicodemus of the Holy Mountain

Men's terrors in face of the enigmatically dangerous universe led them to postulate the existence of angry gods.

Aldous Huxley

And altogether the fear that hovered about me was such an unknown and immense kind of fear, so unlike anything I had ever felt before, that it woke a sense of awe and wonder in me that did much to counteract its worst effects.

Algernon Blackwood

S olomon was wrong: something is new under the sun. More precisely, there are some new sorts of people under the sun — the men and women who call themselves animal-rights activists. It is true that Jains have for over two millennia been vegetarians and opposed to all animal slaughter, and also true that ancient Jews not only did not hunt for sport but also had rules for butchering so as to avoid giving unnecessary pain. But the notion that animals, like people, actually have rights is, to my knowledge, new to the history of ideas. What brought it forth?

The answer is an absence and a presence. The absence is the removal from general purview of animal executions. Most people in our society no longer farm or fish or hunt, nor do they grow up with cows and chickens. In addition, the doors to the slaughterhouse are not open for public viewing: who would ever tour such a place? The result is that while we may still eat meat, we forget or suppress the deaths that make our meals possible. So we are not, unlike those who came before us, hardened to such deaths. Moreover, our amnesia, which spares us unpleasant thoughts, is nourished by the grocery store, which shapes and packages most meats so that any resemblance to living creatures does not obtain. The result — I speak from personal observation of my children — is that a youngster may eat chicken for some time before realizing that the stuff on the plate was once very much alive.

The everyday absence of animals bred for consumption and our decreasing participation in their executions have coincided with — or rather, been replaced by — a novel presence. I refer to the advent of numerous creatures that fall into four broad categories: the toy animal (including especially the stuffed animal), the cartoon figure, the children's book character, and, of course, the ubiquitous household pet — altogether a truly vast menagerie. Never before in history have so many people been so close to so many animals, all of them, it must be emphasized, harmless and friendly, even the crocodiles. The vast majority of these modern animals are the offspring of our own hands and in that sense unreal, without life. But even those that are not unreal, even those that are flesh and blood, such as our indoor cats and fenced-in dogs, do not serve our physical needs. Rather, they are our friends, our companions. We give them names, play games with them, and (sometimes) let them sleep

3

with us. In short, we love them — just as we love, if only a little less, our stuffed animals, our cartoon characters, and the talking animals we see and read about in books. And that love, that affection, is primarily what shapes contemporary attitudes about animals, attitudes only reinforced by visits to the zoo, where even lions and tigers and bears do not much frighten anyone.

In this era after Darwin, in which *Homo sapiens* is just one more member of the order of primates, we are seemingly impelled either to lower ourselves to the level of other animals or to raise them up and deem them our equals. There is, on the one hand, Desmond Morris's *The Naked Ape,* according to which human nature is discovered through the study of monkeys, our near cousins. But there is also, on the other hand, Bill Schull's *Animal Immortality,* which catalogues the evidence for the survival of nonhuman creatures. Although the two books are worlds apart in orientation, in both of them the animals are like us, and we are like the animals. Such is the modern mentality, spawned by both the absence and the presence referred to above.

All this could have been foreseen. If, one hundred years ago, a bright sociologist had been given a prophetic dream in which he beheld a grocery store, a teddy bear, a Looney Tune, and a book by Dr. Seuss, that sociologist would have been fully equipped to predict what we do in fact witness today: an expanding number of vegetarians, an increasing discontent with research on laboratory animals, and a growing tendency to speak of animals as though they were human beings. Our sociologist might even have been able, with sufficient prescience, to foresee the advent (I am not making this up) of 1-800-922-FROG, the toll-free number established to console distraught high-school children who, for anatomy class, must lift a long-dead frog or fetal pig from its glass of cold formaldehyde and cut it to pieces.

The preceding paragraphs should not be construed as criticism of the animal rights movement, whose claims I do not wish to combat here. One does not resolve a philosophical matter by determining what cultural factors have brought it into prominence and made people receptive to it. That would be the genetic fallacy. The point is this: our convictions, however much they may be thought of as the conclusions of arguments, are often heavily indebted to environmental factors we fail to perceive because we are too close to them.

The generalization holds equally for our religious convictions and feelings. An example from another time illustrates the point. In ancient Egypt, Nature was reliable, orderly, and generally benevolent. The Nile gave life to all and always behaved in a predictable fashion. And human beings, at least those belonging to the upper classes, were, insofar as one may judge such things, relatively secure and comfortable. Accordingly, they took themselves to be important members of the universe, a fact reflected in their official mythology and religion.

It was quite otherwise in ancient Mesopotamia, the cradle of the first real civilization. The Tigris and the Euphrates were not so periodic and dependable as the Nile. Flooding had no seasonal rhythm. Mesopotamia was, moreover, continually buffeted by unpredictable dust storms as well as by torrential rains. It is no surprise, then, that people between the rivers did not think as highly of themselves as the Egyptians did. In the great scheme of things, they were obviously not the objects of special care. In accord with this, they thought of the gods as clashing wills, as unpredictable, as not always benevolent. In sum, the harsh, whimsical environment of Mesopotamia, while it did not wholly determine its people's worldview, certainly did shape it and so likewise shape their religion. One recalls that hell is hot for the religions of the dry Middle East but cold in the mythologies of snowy Scandinavia.

What does all this have to do with our own time? A great deal, or so I now wish to argue. We live in a so-called secular society, the surface manifestations of which are well known. Whereas our educational institutions grew out of medieval Christian culture, contemporary public-school curricula are mostly devoid of reference to God. Whereas theology was once the queen of the sciences, today most of the best young minds at our universities choose to study physical sciences, not religion. And whereas, if we leave aside a few ancient Greeks and Romans, it is hard to find any European before Samuel Pepys (1633-1703) given to sincere doubt of God's existence, the percentage of agnostics and atheists among the general populace is today statistically significant.

Now when we inquire why all this should be so, why we should be so different from our forebears, we are usually referred to the history of ideas. Mention will be made, for instance, of Hume's critique of the traditional proofs of the existence of God, of the rise of biblical criticism in nineteenth-century Germany, and of Darwin's theory of evolution, which undid the book of Genesis. Have not new thoughts and discoveries rendered Christianity — and, for that matter, all religions that posit deities and require belief in sacred scriptures — philosophically problematic?

But the tale, while not wholly false, is not wholly true; that is, it is too simple. For arguments always proceed from minds, and minds are never disembodied or disinterested things. What is missing from the standard story, from the usual narrative of the progression of ideas, is the impact of wider environmental factors.

There were, long before Hume, thinkers — Christian thinkers (William of Occam, for instance) — who doubted that Aristotle and Thomas Aquinas had proved the existence of God. The question then is, Why did they retain faith in God while, later on, so many readers of Hume did not? I cannot but surmise that Hume believed as he did, and eventually gained a sympathetic hearing, because his world was already tending toward his heretical conclusions; that is, his contemporaries were predisposed to pay less heed to traditional religious claims.

So too was it later with those who enthusiastically embraced Darwin as a repudiation of Genesis — certainly T. H. Huxley was no unwilling convert, compelled as it were by the evidence against his will — and with those who interpreted modern biblical criticism as a justification for unbelief. As Henry Adams wrote, his contemporaries were already looking for "the very best substitute for religion." Again, why did the Lisbon earthquake cause Voltaire and others to question Christianity while no analogous effect trailed all the evils of the Middle Ages, the Crusades, the plagues, the Turks? Before 1700, misfortune made people doubt firstly themselves, not God and the Christian faith. Obviously, much depends upon our prior inclinations.

My question then is, What accounts for prior inclinations? In particular, what accounts for the medieval tendency to believe, or for the modern tendency to disbelieve?

There can be, of course, no one correct answer. We are confronted here by a confluence of many impulses. History is a mess that cannot be sorted out. But some small part of the truth does, I suggest, come into view when we pull our attention away from philosophers and scientists and theologians, away from debates and books and discoveries, and direct it instead to an obvious yet often overlooked connection: seeming secularization correlates directly with a growing physical separation from the so-called natural world. In other words, the more we have moved indoors, the less some of us have been inclined to believe. Reflection soon reveals that this fact is neither uninteresting nor mysterious. There are several good and manifest reasons why this should be the case. Let me begin with the concept of wonder.

Socrates, according to Plato in the *Theaetetus,* maintained that philosophy has no foundation other than the feeling of wonder. Aristotle later concurred, and in so doing went on to instance, as the chief objects of wonder, the moon, the sun, and the stars. Now it could also be said that religion, like philosophy, begins with wonder, or at least that religion without wonder is dead. This observation presents us with our problem.

In the past, the stars over our heads have nurtured human wonder as much as anything else, or perhaps more than anything else. The impact upon the collective psyche of the tiny sparkles overhead, together with the sun and the moon, would be hard to overestimate, although this fact is hard for us moderns to appreciate fully. Our traditional mythologies, our poetry, our fiction — all are filled with stories about the heavenly bodies, which have been from the beginning a preoccupation of the human mind. Indeed, astral religion and the fallacy known as astrology, whose relics are unfortunately still with us, have found a home among many peoples, as has the concept of astral immortality, according to which human beings can become stars. And — as we have lately learned — what is Stonehenge but a monument to the heavens?

Why? What explains our long-standing obsession with the lights above us? The stark beauty of the heavens is obviously part of the reason.

But more important is the stars' endless ability to fascinate: they are things always beyond our grasp, things we can see but never touch. All we can do — or rather, all we were able to do until recent times — is tell stories, and wonder:

> The stars sing an anthem of glory
>   I cannot put into speech.

Robert William Service

Today, however, awareness of the sky and its lights is much less a part of our everyday consciousness. Most people are asleep when the sun comes up and inside a building when it sets; and when they do venture outside at night, there are too many artificial lights for them to see stars. In my experience, people in the city rarely satisfy their sparse curiosity about the heavens by raising their eyes. Instead they visit a planetarium. I myself have spent some time looking into a cardboard tube called "Cosmos" while lying on my bed: the clever instrument lets me see the constellations without going outside. I recall one occasion when I impressed a man by locating for him the North Star and the Big Dipper, as though knowledge of such were arcane, the province of the learned.

But it is not just the absence of certain astronomical facts from our minds that characterizes us. As the stars belong less and less to our direct experience, our very hearts are made different from the hearts of those who came before us. Not only have our shelters and omnipresent lights permitted us fewer moments of wonder under the stars; they have also surely fostered a diminishment in our collective ability to wonder. Despite our ignoring the fact, the retreat of the stars has not been trivial.

What does religion lose? For one thing, it loses its best illustration of the concept of transcendence; for the stars are the one irrefutable proof (and, in the past, the one constant reminder) that there are things of whose existence we may know but whose nature ever escapes our knowledge. For another, the stars, as Aristotle affirmed, and as Kant later agreed, are the strongest natural stimuli to wonder, and wonder nurtures religious feelings and reflections. Consider Psalm 136:3-9:

O give thanks to the Lord of lords, for his steadfast love endures for ever; to him who alone does great wonders, for his steadfast love endures for ever; to him who by understanding made the heavens, for his steadfast love endures for ever; to him who spread out the earth upon the waters, for his steadfast love endures for ever; to him who made the great lights, for his steadfast love endures for ever; the sun to rule over the day, for his steadfast love endures for ever; the moon and stars to rule over the night, for his steadfast love endures for ever.

This text was written by an individual who knew the stars, and behind it there is an experience with which many could not now identify. When Paul wrote that "ever since the creation of the world his [God's] invisible nature, namely, his eternal power and deity, has been clearly perceived in the things that have been made" (Rom. 1:20), surely he had the night sky in his mind's eye, as did the psalmist who wrote, "The heavens are telling the glory of God; and the firmament proclaims his handiwork" (Ps. 19:1). But if so, what happens when "the things that have been made" are no longer inescapable objects of vision? (I wonder whether the modern interest in UFOs might be partly due to a continuing need to find mystery above our heads.)

So far I have referred only to the night sky. But there are obviously a thousand additional ways in which the natural world impels us to wonder: the transformation of the caterpillar to chrysalis (a word, incidentally, that young people no longer know because they do not know the thing) to butterfly; the annual migrations of geese; the flashes from lightning bugs in the summer twilight; the intricate webs of spiders; the never-ending activity of ants determined to pile up particles of sand around the entrance to an underground realm. These all open our eyes with wonder and introduce us to other worlds about which we know so little.

Beyond, moreover, the sheer experiences of wonder, there are the endless, enjoyable queries posed to our curious minds. By what secret push-or-pull mechanism does water travel against gravity from the roots of a large tree to its top? How do climbing plants on a wall infallibly manage to grow toward the nearest nail? How do birds flying in formation seemingly manage to change direction synchronously? Nicodemus of the Holy Mountain wrote,

> When the mind contemplates these things [heaven and earth], it marvels and is filled with wonder and rejoices with inexpressible gladness for having such a God and Lord who created with such ease, such beautiful and wise and great and marvelous creatures. So we are moved and say with David: "I praise thee, for thou art beautiful and wonderful. Wonderful are thy works" (Psalm 138:4).

Compare the more subdued, less religious, but still analogous words of Charles Darwin:

> I cannot be contented to view this wonderful universe, and especially the nature of man, and to conclude that everything is the result of brute force. I am inclined to look at everything as resulting from designed laws, with the details, whether good or bad, left to the working out of what we may call chance. Not that this notion *at all* satisfies me. I feel most deeply that the whole subject is too profound for the human intellect. A dog might as well speculate on the mind of Newton. Let each man hope and believe what he can.

Nature, even everyday Nature close to home, is full of wonderful mysteries, that is, mysteries that make us wonder — to whose number modern biology has added much more than it has subtracted. Nature is not a singularity but a plurality, a host to multiple worlds; and intimacy with it teaches what is a fundamental presupposition of authentic religion: that there is much beyond our vision. Without such intimacy, that fundamental presupposition is perhaps not so readily intuited.

If an increasing distance from Nature has cut us off from multitudinous sources of wonder, it has also cut us off from certain feelings of terror and replaced them with nurtured feelings of self-sufficiency, even complacency. In the face of earthquakes and tornados, our parents were helpless. Droughts and floods left them humbled, cognizant of their own impotence. But the more we construct buildings that will survive earthquakes, the more we learn about predicting tornados in time to take shelter, the more we think about seeding clouds and towing icebergs, and the more we build drainage ditches to divert floods, the less terrified we become. This is so important because those who are terrified always cry out for help, just as those who are not terrified can remain confident in themselves.

The psychology is inevitable, and problematic for the heirs of Paul and Augustine. For Christianity has always posited that we cannot solve our own problems, at least our profoundest problems. Rather, something is wrong with human beings, so wretchedly wrong that matters cannot be made right without divine intervention, or what we call God's grace. The Christian message — whose sponsors have sometimes spoken of "election" and "predestination" to underline our utter feebleness — presupposes feelings of helplessness and sin. It presupposes that we cannot save ourselves, that certain matters are out of our hands.

In the past this presupposition was not troublesome. Our feelings about God were roughly congruent with our feelings about Nature. Often terrified and helpless before the one, we often felt terrified and helpless before the other. But increasing physical security, our withdrawal from storms and from "Nature, red in tooth and claw," has altered our feelings about the world, thereby altering our feelings about ourselves and, in line with that, our feelings about God. Surely the modern dismissal of hell stems partly from an increasing lack of direct contact with Nature's indifference and darkness. As the example of the old Egyptians shows, a friendly Nature begets a friendly God. And we are in the process of making Nature friendly. Certainly that is what countless fishing trips and family vacations accomplish.

Despite what I've just said, it is a modern irony that the increasing insulation of human beings has done much less to make people happy than one might have expected. Economic man, to use Philip Rieff's phrase, thought that if lower needs were attended to, a general satisfaction of the higher needs would follow. But we have learned what William Blake, that despiser of scientific progress, long ago knew with intuitive certainty: that relative health and safety do not of themselves generate contentment. Human beings are too needy to be satisfied by physical well-being. Nonetheless, even in the midst of our manifest sins, patent failures, and obvious needs, our increasing control of the environment has left a collective illusion of self-sufficiency and mastery. Now perhaps it is harder to bend the knees of the heart. Industrialization, despite its many attendant miseries and the consequent lamentations, and despite the protests of the Romantic poets and others, has left in its wake a self-centered confidence in human beings. Even all the horrors of the twentieth century have not undone this confidence.

Consider in this connection the current proliferation of self-help books. How do we account for this? The existence of such books clearly reflects widespread recognition of our need for help: something is wrong and needs to be made right. But the myth is that we ourselves are up to the task: the help is to be self-help. We fail to fathom that the very act of buying a self-help book is, from one point of view, a contradiction, for it is an admission that we must call upon another for assistance. The contradiction is paradigmatic. Our consciousness of collective scientific powers and technological successes occludes our awareness of individual incapacity and personal problems. The ongoing mastery of Nature, which is in effect removal from Nature, has reduced the habit of feeling helpless, a habit which was once, on a subconscious level, congruent with the Christian mission.

There is a third way in which withdrawal from the natural world has perhaps dampened certain religious feelings. For centuries now there has been movement from countryside to city. Economic changes and technological advances have allowed masses to live in close quarters, so that crowds are met with everywhere. The result is that we have inflation, an

inflation of people, too many people in one place. I say too many because inflation always devalues. The more dollar bills in circulation, the
less their value. We esteem what is rare. Were the world's population of
houseflies suddenly to plummet to seven, our attitude toward them
would instantly change: we would highly esteem them and take steps to
ensure their survival. And people would line up to see them. But as soon
as they multiplied once more to become ubiquitous, we would again
have no qualms about squashing them.

It is just so with people. In the dark film *The Third Man,* Orson
Welles's evil character looks from atop a giant Ferris wheel at the human
specks below and comments that from his perspective they are small and
many and accordingly worthless, so killing them would be no crime.
Massive urbanization tends to breed analogous sentiments, which is perhaps one reason why murder rates are so high in the cities: there people
are less valued. We need only call to mind Jack the Ripper's East End
London.

Many years ago there was a poll of scientists. Its object was to gauge
belief in God. As it turned out, not too many acknowledged a supreme
being. But of those that did, there was a significantly higher percentage
of cosmologists than biologists, and a significantly higher percentage of
biologists than psychologists. In other words, the closer one's profession
took one toward human beings, the less belief there was. These findings
are not surprising. Despite all the wonderful things one can say about us,
the litany of our evils is long; our sins are piled high to heaven. It is only
natural that so many early Christians entered the desert — they found it
easier to practice Christianity without anyone else around.

But we are doing the opposite of what the early anchorites and cenobites did. We are emptying the wilderness and filling the cities. The upshot is that, like the psychologists with their steady stream of patients,
we experience human inflation and (with the persistent aid of the media)
confront more human ills and evils than we can bear. As we come closer
and closer to ourselves, we become uncertain and cynical. In such a context it is surely much less natural to believe in the infinite worth of a human soul, or to imagine that we are all passionately loved by an invisible
spirit. Our preoccupation with what is called "self-esteem" only shows

that we do not have any. The psalmist asked, "Whither shall I flee from thy presence?" (Ps. 139:7, KJV). One good answer is, inside a house in the city.

The direction of my argument must not be misunderstood. Surely those who tan themselves in the summer sun are not more religious than others; and I hesitate to embrace the old Jeffersonian notion that those who live in the country must be more virtuous than the rest of us. My point instead concerns general attitudes and predispositions. Experience of the natural world does not generate faith. (Christianity is not a so-called Nature religion.) But surely it can encourage a certain psychological orientation favorable to some brands of religious faith; and this suggests the correlative possibility that reduced experience of the natural world might do just the opposite.

When Peter stood up on the day of Pentecost, he did not have to start from scratch. His audience already believed in God, a Messiah, the Resurrection. It was simply a question of whether God had in fact raised Jesus, proving him to be Israel's Messiah. But preachers today increasingly share less and less with a secular audience. Belief in God, a Messiah, and a life beyond can no longer be taken for granted. Only a Tertullian, with his divorce between Athens and Jerusalem, between secular human reason and divine revelation, could fail to be disturbed by this. Adolf Harnack wrote, "The most important step . . . ever taken in the domain of Christian doctrine was when the apologists at the beginning of the second century drew the equation: the Logos = Jesus." We, however, live in a world without an analogous equation, so that the center of the Christian faith is no longer intelligible to many. But the problem goes even deeper, beyond beliefs to general feelings and attitudes. How do we preach the good news to those who, because they pass the time indoors, have rarely wondered at the stars or been terrified before storms; to those who, because of human congregating and its attendant psychological effects, are inclined to think themselves of little worth; to those who, because of technological advances, are predisposed to associate salvation with self-help and science? Those who preach while unaware of these questions can only wonder why many in their audience grow ever more suspicious. Christians may claim that Jesus Christ is the same yesterday, today, and forever. But the rest of us are not.

Urbanization and our move indoors have even brought about a distancing of ourselves from Scripture, although most of us are oblivious to this fact. Just as high school students who read Chaucer no longer laugh at Chanticleer because they no longer know anything about the behavior of roosters, so too is the Bible becoming foreign to us, who now pass most of our time in artificial environments. I surely speak for many in saying that few of the significant events in my life have taken place outdoors. It was just the opposite for Jesus. Almost every important event in his life occurred outside — his baptism, his temptation, his transfiguration, his entry into Jerusalem, his crucifixion. The clouds and orbs in the sky were his roof (and I recall that when he spoke of the Last Things, he saw the Son of Man coming on the clouds of heaven and the stars falling from the sky). The fact is hermeneutically relevant. One wonders: Is the story of Adam and Eve not less memorable for people who have spent almost no time in real gardens? Is it not likely that the rhetorical resonance of Jesus' agricultural parables is dulled for readers who require every detail about planting and harvesting to be explained? Can those who run to sturdy shelters when tornado sirens sound fully appreciate the terror of the disciples on the waves of a stormy Sea of Galilee? Can people who do not know the difference between a sparrow and a starling have any deep emotional response to Jesus' command to "look at the birds of the air" (Matt. 6:26)? It is hard enough — or rather, close to impossible — to cross the chronological and geographical spaces; but when we have also quitted the natural world, is it not harder to feel sympathy for the characters in the Bible and to identify with their stories? This too is troubling.

Our problems, I anticipate, will only be exacerbated as the future comes toward us. Particularly worrisome is the advent of what is called virtual reality, the new technology that will allow people to deceive their senses utterly, to stimulate their brain centers to experience as real the totally unreal. Virtual reality, imposed by a helmet over the head, is artificial experience plugged directly into the brain. Its proponents tell us that, not far from now, we will be able to construct scenarios and immerse our minds in them without physical risk or harm. When the thing finally enters the home, we will no longer passively watch: we will make our fictions fact. Many of those fictions will obviously be sexual: people will no longer fantasize over self-generated pictures in their heads but rather live out their imaginings with preprogrammed, non-existent partners who in every way seem real. The proliferation of pornography on the Internet is a preview of things to come.

Virtual reality will of course bring many apparent blessings. I for one am looking forward to "traveling" to places I could not otherwise visit and to looking at buildings and pieces of art I could not otherwise examine. I will be thrilled to study the *Mona Lisa,* visit Hagia Sophia, and joust with Robin Hood, all the while never leaving my living room. But what will result when the light of the TV, which has replaced the glow of the campfire, is itself eclipsed by virtual reality? TV is tempting enough for most people. Virtual reality will be well nigh irresistible. It does not require prophetic imagination to envision vast numbers of human beings organizing life around virtual-reality adventures. Given the opportunity, the human ostrich will undoubtedly spend as much time as possible with its head in the fascinating sands of virtual reality. The withdrawal from Nature will then be all the closer to completion.

Closer to completion, but only closer. Virtual reality will itself undoubtedly be just one more stage on the way. Not long ago I read an article in a science magazine on the prospects for artificial immortality. The author, who took himself to be detailing utopia, not a nightmare, contended that the brain and spinal cord will someday be removed from the body, hooked up to sophisticated computers and video equipment, and then encased in a concrete bunker. The only problem is that cerebral tissue ages in seven or eight hundred years. That difficulty, however, can be overcome by keeping a supply of sperm and eggs on hand: every few centuries one need only fertilize an ovum, let it grow a few weeks, then graft its virgin brain tissue onto the elder, disembodied brain, and all will be well.

Whether this contemporary version of the Dracula myth is our future I do not pretend to know. But that the prospect outlined is desired by some among us speaks worlds. Paradise was once thought of as a garden. Now it can be a concrete box. The hope for immortality once involved, in the words of Daniel, being "like the stars for ever and ever" (Dan. 12:3). Today it can be union with earthbound electronic equipment.

Human beings bear the divine image, and the imperative upon them is to imitate their Creator, that good Spirit who rains upon the just and the unjust. But in our age it is the other way around. We, the creators, imitate the things we have created. Enthralled by the machines we have made, we think of ourselves in mechanistic terms — modern psychology texts are filled with numbers that quantify human behavior — and try to turn ourselves into the most efficient and longest-lasting machines we can be. That we translate the successes of our athletes into statistics is paradigmatic. Such is the logical conclusion of the human withdrawal from the natural world.

A few observations on natural theology are perhaps pertinent here. I refer to the old natural theology, which reflected upon the natural world. This was not, against the textbook explanation, simply laid to rest by Darwin and his much-overdone exposure of the never-ending struggle for existence, nor by Barth and his mocking of insectotheology and like excesses. It died also in large part because the theologians moved indoors, thereby cutting themselves off from their traditional sources of inspiration. Natural theology without Nature lost its traditional potency.

Further, the theological abandonment of the natural world, the handing over of it to the scientists, meant the sundering of the sacred and the secular, with the result that the theologians immediately found themselves in a cultural ghetto, addressing only souls at a moment in history when the very existence of souls had come to be doubted.

Rudolf Bultmann, the true heir of Descartes, is here the great lesson. His existentialism directly related God to nothing at all in the world at large, which is why his audience was made up entirely of theologians and church members. Bultmann ended up proclaiming an isolated word, a word isolated from both Nature and culture, isolated from everything save the church. But there is no future in that. Without *vistiga Dei in mondo* there is no *Deus*.

The church at this point in history does not need another Augustinian personal theology, nor can Schleiermacher be the way to the future. We need instead what natural theology once supplied: a way of relating God to our environment. But the theologians have been worrying about other things.

There is, one may be surprised to learn, an entire book dedicated to explaining what the brilliant third-century church father Origen thought about the stars. But one could not, I would wager, write even an article on what any theologian since Paley, who died in 1805, has had to say on the subject. The night sky has disappeared from theology.

Kafka lamented, "God lies outside our existence." That is our pressing predicament, and one less frequently felt when people lived closer to the creation. For then God was felt to be directly related not just to souls but also to the environment in which people inevitably carried on their lives. But with the proliferation of artificial environments, the Divinity has become related almost exclusively to souls, and God's relationship to the inorganic world in which we live, the world of artificial environments, is now problematic. One understands why the old cosmological and teleological arguments have fallen upon hard times. The feelings that once motivated their construction, feelings engendered by prolonged contemplation of the natural world, are not so prevalent.

Let me approach my conclusion with a series of propositions. First, technological progress, although it includes much that is not progress, probably cannot be halted or even slowed. The prophetic voices of such as Thomas Berry, Jacques Ellul, and Neil Postman will, despite their speaking much truth, continue to draw only small crowds. Our growing isolation from Nature is an inevitable result of the universal human condition. We dislike suffering and enjoy comfort, and to the extent that

Nature brings suffering, to that extent will we distance ourselves from it; and to the extent that artificial environments bring comfort, to that extent will we place ourselves in them. Even Scripture itself looks forward to a time when the sun will not beat upon us (Rev. 21:23). Whenever technology promises comfort (as it always has and always will: that is its *raison d'être*), it will be allowed free rein — even if its promises are, as so often, bogus.

Our current condition is vividly illustrated by this, that nothing is more dead than the old Roman Stoicism of Epictetus and Marcus Aurelius; indeed, it is so far from being practicable that, as those of us who have tried to teach modern college students something about the history of philosophy well know, it can no longer even be understood. Perhaps one might take some solace in the prophetic speculation of T. S. Eliot: "The indefinite elaboration of scientific discovery and invention . . . may reach a point at which there will be an irresistible revulsion of humanity and a readiness to accept the most primitive hardships rather than carry any longer the burden of modern civilization." But is this not unjustified optimism?

Second, attempts to spend more time in "the great outdoors" will accomplish little. Certainly the church retreat — a mostly modern phenomenon that was not needed when people were closer to the natural world — will no more effect change in the churches than the Boy Scout weekend — again something for which there was no call before we all moved indoors. Our withdrawal to the great indoors has altered the face of our society. People in the Western world, although they may enjoy public parks, are now and forever indoor creatures, with all the psychological changes that brings. This is one reason why the recent calls to revive the cult of the earth mother are probably naïve: the goddess, estranged from Nature, may never be much more than a mask for political interests.

Third, there is a pressing need for serious reflection on just what psychological changes technology has wrought in us. What are the ramifications of our immersion in technology, and how do they affect religion? Has the ubiquity of portable timepieces in any way altered conceptions of time and eternity? Does artificial lighting in every nook and cranny make the distinction between darkness and light less important and so subtly change our response to what have traditionally been the outstanding symbols of good and evil? What does the habit of rapidly switching TV channels with a remote-control device do to the virtue of patience? How has the removal of flickering candles from sanctuaries and the substitution of electric bulbs with their harsh, steady light changed the moods of worshippers? There are myriads of such questions that are rarely asked but clearly significant. Yet our pastors and theologians — who nowadays speak so readily about the goodness of creation and yet seem unaware that the constant and inevitable raising of air-conditioned, artificially lighted church buildings might be interpreted as an ironic parable, an unconscious participation in the flight from heaven and earth, an unwitting repudiation of "And God saw that it was good" — are not of much aid here. They have of late reflected much on ecology, but that is an altogether different subject.

Fourth, one doubts that science itself will any time soon make up our lack. To be sure, both biology and space exploration have uncovered and will continue to uncover new worlds of wonder; and the cosmologists have given us the so-called anthropic principle, which raises teleological questions. So perhaps we should take solace. But the worlds of the astrophysicist and the biologist and the cosmologist will remain, for the foreseeable future, well known only to the specialists. They accordingly cannot supply the rest of us with the sort of direct and continual confrontation with wonder that might affect the collective psyche.

Perhaps one might hope, as did Frank Lloyd Wright, that technology will reverse urbanization. As machines increasingly replace physical labor, jobs will necessarily become more and more knowledge-based, so, one might imagine, the omnipresence of electronic devices for the transmission of information will eliminate the need to congregate in the city. As of now, however, we have only the suburbs that have been brought to us by the automobile; and even if masses were to move out beyond them, even if we were to witness a return to the countryside, the artificial environments would go with us. Only a little would be gained. Augustine's conversion in a garden and Ignatius of Loyola's *eximia ilustración* while gazing at a stream stand for the past, not the present.

Finally, cataphatic theology, in the sense of Pseudo-Dionysius —

namely, constructing analogies for God from the things of the natural world — is no longer a preoccupation of theologians. But some sort of substitution for it must be found. Early Christianity overcame Gnosticism by proclaiming God the creator of the cosmos, and it satisfied Hellenistic rationalism by making its own the Stoic Logos. In these ways it related itself not only to the heart but also to the mind and to the environment, that is, the natural world, and it understood God in terms of all three. Nothing less is required of theology today. God, to be God for us, must be linked to the world around us. I recall in this connection a delightful passage from Martin Buber's *Tales of the Hasidim:*

> "You can learn something from everything," the rabbi of Sadagora once said to his hasidim. "Everything can teach us something, and not only everything God has created. What man has made also has something to teach us." "What can we learn from a train?" one hasid asked dubiously. "That because of one second one can miss everything." "And from the telegraph?" "That every word is counted and charged." "And from the telephone?" "That what we say here is heard there."

Would that it were so easy. Despite the edifying observations of the rabbi of Sadagora, one is at a loss to relate God in any direct or profound way to technology as such or to our modern environment. That environment is the sundry collection of artificial cubicles in which we pass our time. Our houses and automobiles are filled with comforts and distractions. It is probable that no one has yet created a cataphatic theology grounded in technological analogies because it cannot be done. Technological artifacts point us to the wrong creator — to the human race, not God; so they seem bereft of real signals of transcendence. Further, as they become our environment, they imprint in the collective subconscious the message that things exist in order to serve us. That is the very last thing we need to intuit.

The manifold attempts of religious apologists to discover points of convergence between beliefs of scientists and traditional Christian doctrine — between, for instance, the so-called Big Bang and Genesis I —

are, moreover, here irrelevant. This is first because scientists constantly change their minds about everything. Today's assured result is tomorrow's refuted hypothesis. (I for one would not be surprised to see the Big Bang theory discarded someday.) Second, discovery of convergences still does nothing about the effects of the environment upon us.

But where then does that leave us? The problems, unfortunately, are much more vivid than any answers. There are times when I, of little faith, doubt that there are any satisfactory solutions. Perhaps we will, if spared a cultural apocalypse, indeed end up as a race of Draculas. Perhaps our fate is to go unconsciously wherever technology leads us: what can be done will be done. Certainly that is what seems to be occurring at the present time. There is, so to speak, no pope to outlaw the crossbow, no ethical force to direct the technological march. And so we are, without being aware of it, constantly being remade by the products of our own hands. But into what no one really knows. As we change our environment, our environment changes us, and in many more ways than I have indicated here or even could indicate. The complexity of things is beyond all of us.

One can, in view of all I have said, wonder whether religion has a significant role left to play in a secular world. But surely it does. The religious we always have with us. Here the Andrew Greeleys are right. Although increased unbelief, widespread relativism, and large structures independent of religion, such as big government, big business, big education, and big entertainment, are here to stay, human beings will forever ask questions of meaning; and religion, including the traditional major religions, will always help many find their answers. Certainly we are not, if polls and statistics are any guide, on an inevitable march to a truly secular world.

And yet the environmental factors I have discussed will probably retard in some the germination of certain religious thoughts and sentiments and maybe in others help stunt or kill them altogether. So even apart from all the purely intellectual objections that the modern world has thrown at Christianity, the religious spirit may now grow in less productive soil.

My late father fought in the Second World War as an enlisted man. He told me that he discovered what he was up to only after he returned home and read a few books. In the midst of battle, ignorance and confusion governed. Knowledge consisted of concrete imperatives: go left, retreat, hold your fire, cross the bridge, walk the road, take the town. How his deeds furthered some master plan he knew not: there was for him no big picture. My father could not see the forest because he was a tree. He just followed orders and tried to stay alive.

Those of us who are religious are like my father. We know that we are in a war but not how it goes or how it will eventuate; and few of us are generals. Our lot is rather to be good soldiers — to live according to the imperatives upon us and to save our souls. For this reason, then, the chapters of this book do not contain social prescriptions. My purpose is not to move the river but to navigate it, and on occasion to land the boat. In other words, I wish, through analysis of the past and the present, to share certain thoughts with those who do not want to be unwittingly carried downstream by the things around us.

STILLNESS

CHAPTER 1

Mute Angels

Simeon ben Gamaliel said: "All my days have I grown up among the sages, and I have found nothing better for a man than silence."

Mishnah Aboth

Abba Theophilus, the archbishop, came to Scetis one day. The brethren who were assembled said to Abba Pambo, "Say something to the archbishop, so that he may be edified." The old man said to them: "If he is not edified by my silence, he will not be edified by my speech."

Apophthegmata Patrum

Among the angels there is no place for outward, but only for inward speech.

Thomas Aquinas

W hen Jack's mother threw her son's beans out the window, her intent was not to induce the adventure that followed. And when Odysseus crossed the Aegean to rescue an abducted queen, he did not envisage two decades of woe. And when the wife in O. Henry's "The Gift of the Magi" cut her hair, sold it, and bought her husband a fob chain for his treasured watch, she had no idea he would sell that watch and with his profit purchase the set of jeweled combs she craved.

All memorable and well-crafted narratives are, as a rule, full of surprises; this is so because their characters (and so too their readers) never know exactly what the upshot of a particular action will be. The line from Luke, "they know not what they do," belongs to the plot of every satisfying story. Those within a narrative never behold the future, for their acts always produce chains of unanticipated consequences. In all this, however, art is simply mimesis, the imitation of life. What chaos theory tells us about the weather, and what the Austrian school of economics teaches us about monetary markets, holds for the story of every human being: any system with a sufficient number of variables is too complex to be controlled, and its future states cannot be precisely forecast.

One recalls that the French mathematician Laplace, like the Stoics and Leibniz before him, imagined that an omniscient being could, from comprehensive knowledge of the universe at any point in time, predict its entire future in encyclopedic detail. But even were one to embrace a materialistic determinism and agree with Laplace that all is exhaustively predetermined, the unalterable circumstance would remain: we are not omniscient. Thus the morrow remains for us indistinct. This is why soothsayers, who prefer dim light and (if wise) suffuse their forecasts with ambiguity, will always be with us. What they claim to do simply cannot be done, so the demand for their services is never sated.

Because every human life in particular is filled with — or rather, constituted by — unintended consequences, the same is true of history in general. Indeed, this last is the record of human beings coming to terms with the unanticipated effects of earlier actions. Put otherwise, history is the containment of accidents. How better to characterize the division of the world upon the death of Alexander the Great, or the flurry of activity after Columbus's discovery of the New World, or the entry of nations into World War I? Nonetheless, our divine instinct to bring order out of chaos often obscures this fact and moves us to descry logic within history's irrational course. In this way we can wrongly interpret unintended effects as once-conscious aims — as though Luther, when he nailed his ninety-five theses to the door of Wittenberg castle, envisioned Protestantism. It is like the man who unwittingly cracks a joke and then takes credit for it, misleading others into thinking him clever. We repeatedly credit famous names with too much power, as if some of them actually intended the consequences of their deeds and so truly held the reins of history. But none did; and those presumptuous enough to think themselves exceptions have only been like the hard-hearted Pharaoh of the Exodus, whose decisions were not his own ("God hardened Pharaoh's heart").

As with history, so too with the so-called history of ideas. The stars of philosophers rise and fall, and trends of thought come and go, and all is explained as the orderly outcome of argument. But arguments can be rationalizations, effects masquerading as causes. Marx was justified in supposing that ideas are not always the engine of history, and that concentration upon thinkers and their thoughts sometimes obscures powerful, irrational forces: not everything important can be adjusted to what Descartes called "the level of reason." Just such a concentration has, however, deceived many of us with regard to one of the chief circumstances of the last few centuries, that being the modern advance of science and its coincidence with a retreat — not as broad as some think, but a retreat nonetheless — of religion.

Science presently rules our culture as religion once did. It is natural to infer that, as we have all been taught, there must be a causal connection between the decline of the old and the ascent of the new. Have not the many wounds of religion been largely inflicted by a hostile science? Have not the beliefs and attitudes often fostered by the latter, beliefs and attitudes roundly understood to be inconsistent with the faith and practice of religious people, carried the day and in the process brought into being the secular society in which we now live? Such questions can only be rhetorical, for the historical course of events is plain enough. Despite some reasonable voices protesting that this need not be so, science has not nourished religion, and no one can suppose otherwise. There remains, however, an all-important matter for reflection. Precisely by what method has religion been laid so low? Here the issue of conscious aim versus unintended consequences is relevant.

It is typically supposed that the grand conflict between science and religion has been an intellectual debate, and that the apparent victory of the one over the other has taken place in the gladiatorial arena of ideas. Science has said one thing, religion another, and the intellectual community, compelled by the facts, has believed science. Our current situation is accordingly the outcome of an argument. Cosmologists, for example, have contended that the world was not created in six twenty-four-hour periods, while biologists have urged that the story of a primeval individual created from the dust of the earth is problematic when the evidence for evolution is dispassionately considered. As a consequence, many no longer understand the first three chapters of Genesis literally, or even pay them heed at all. Science the victor, religion the vanquished.

As I observed in the introductory chapter, I doubt whether this straightforward analysis should be so straightforward. Apart from the fact that Ambrose and other church fathers interpreted parts of Genesis in a figurative fashion, Christian theology has historically been quite capable of reconciling itself to new ideas or modes of thinking. The story of the church's first few centuries is, after all, in part the story of the translation of popular Jewish conceptions into Greek philosophical categories; and the creativity of the great Christian thinkers from that period, as well as from later periods, cannot be denied. Christianity, blessed with the likes of Origen and Thomas Aquinas, has shown itself to be quite adroit at contemplating its teachings under the light of new knowledge. One is skeptical that Christian theology is utterly incapable of domesticating the firm results of modern science.

In this connection I may observe that contemporary historians have unearthed abundant materials showing that early modern science, far from establishing itself in opposition to religious doctrine, was actually nourished by late medieval and Reformation theologies. The truth may be that science itself has propagated a dubious tale about its origins. But that aside, and whatever one makes of the much ballyhooed conflict between the doctrines of science and the dogmas of religion, serious attention needs to be paid to another matter. For science is not a disembodied collection of abstract propositions that may or may not raise questions for faith. Like the Platonic forms, it is manifested in the material world.

The theory of relativity may have been conceived in Einstein's mind as a series of mathematical propositions, but, as one cause in a nexus of causes, it eventually clothed itself in fire and a mushroom cloud. And this is how it goes with so much of science, which has put into our open hands its many inventions. Technology has, in fact, overcrowded our world. Wherever we go, wherever we look, its children come into view.

What does all this have to do with the fate of Christianity? Alasdair MacIntyre has urged that secularization was sired not by overwhelming reasoning but by the effects, wholly unplanned, of urbanization and industrialization. He is largely correct. Secularization is one of history's accidents. It is not the inevitable outcome of dispassionate reasoning and progress in knowledge. The arguments of deists, agnostics, and atheists have won the day in some quarters partly because many, due to the psychological impact of certain environmental changes, have been predisposed toward unbelief. It is perhaps the sociologist, not the philosopher, who can best explain religion's seeming degeneration in certain quarters.

Urbanization and industrialization are, moreover, only two among many environmental factors that have perhaps fostered some apathy for or hostility toward religion. In the preceding chapter I contended that, for instance, a decreasing capacity to wonder and an increasing distance from nature's terrors, both results of moving indoors, have altered our religious dispositions in ways that make reception of the Christian message less intuitive. In this chapter I shall examine yet another current circumstance — the ubiquity of artificial noise — which, when rightly understood, furthers the case that our religious plight is not solely the upshot of science, understood in terms of the history of ideas, but also the inadvertent consequence of technology, understood as the ongoing production of countless things that have radically transformed our world.

I commence with the concept of divertissement, which was so keenly analyzed by the seventeenth-century philosopher and mathematician Blaise Pascal. This profound and devout French Roman Catholic reflected much on the paradoxical human creature and its puzzling condition. Consider this paragraph from Pascal's *Pensées:*

> Is not the royal dignity sufficiently great in itself to make its possessor happy by the mere contemplation of what he is? Must he be diverted from this thought like ordinary folk? I see well that a man is made happy by diverting him from the view of his domestic sorrows so as to occupy all his thoughts with the care of dancing well. But will it be the same with a king, and will he be happier in the pursuit of these idle amusements than in the contemplation of his greatness? And what more satisfactory object could be present to his mind? Would it not be a deprivation of his delight for him to occupy his soul with the thought of how to adjust his steps to the cadence of an air, or of how to throw a ball skillfully, instead of leaving it to enjoy quietly the contemplation of the majestic glory which encompasses him? Let us make the trial; let us leave a king all alone to reflect on himself quite at leisure, without any gratification of the senses, without any care in his mind, without society; and we will see that a king without diversion is a man full of wretchedness. So this is carefully avoided, and near the persons of kings there never fail to be a great number of people who see to it that amusement follows business, and who watch all the time of their leisure to supply them with delights and games, so that there is no blank in it. In fact, kings are surrounded with persons who are wonderfully attentive in taking care that the king be not alone in a state to think of himself, knowing well that he will be miserable, king though he be, if he meditate on self.

These lines help us interpret our world.

People seek divertissement. As a general rule they do not wish to be alone, to contemplate themselves, to deprive the senses. Indeed, the disposition of our species is such that a human being, placed in a sensory deprivation tank, will almost inevitably hallucinate. Those familiar with the work of John Lilly know just how full and colorful such experience can be. When the mind is not entertained, when it encounters no stimuli, it does a fine job of entertaining itself, resurrecting phantoms to dance before the inner eye. We cannot bear darkness, silence, stillness. We crave movement, sound, activity. We do not climb the mountain because it is there but because we are otherwise bored.

I suppose — here I depart from Pascal — that the chief cause of our restlessness is a deep-seated biological pestering intended to benefit us. Without stimuli, the human being does not reach its physiological *telos*. Children who hear no language before their tenth year will never learn to speak; for disuse, the correlate of no excitation, breeds decay. For the same reason, the one born blind for want of corneas cannot, if too much time has passed, ever learn to see, even if healthy corneas are implanted. Without early stimulation, certain structures in the eye and brain never develop. And as in the beginning, so too at life's end: the mind usually does not go bad from age but from disuse: deterioration fills stimulation's lack. Obviously, then, it is a very good thing that we are programmed to seek external stimuli. So too, however, is it good to eat, which does not mean that it is good to overeat. Stimulation is analogous: there can be too much of the good thing. That is why we must ponder Pascal.

When Pascal composed his book of thoughts, his illustration of divertissement was so apt because the king's every wish was command. Royalty was able to surround itself at all times with entertainers, able to work or play without cessation, until sleep called. And with what result? The king feasted, played croquet, and amused himself with rowdy guests. Tranquility was evaded, no void allowed. Activity prevailed. No one else, however, had the resources to carry on quite like the king. Pascal therefore fittingly offered the king as the paradigm of the human being seeking divertissement.

It is altogether different in these latter days. With the development of assorted technologies, devices of distraction have become ubiquitous. Everybody now owns televisions, radios, CD players. The outcome? People behave as did the kings of old, using the new equipment to shun sensory deprivation. Pascal might have foretold it. Human nature abhors a vacuum. It is restless and carries within itself a strong desire for activity, a powerful instinct to seek amusement, to gratify itself through treating its sensory organs to stimuli from external sources. Technology has been manipulated accordingly, to produce machines of stimulation, gadgets for divertissement. It is as if the function once served by the king's attendants is currently fulfilled by our ever-multiplying entertainment devices. To put it succinctly: Whether sitting before a television or jogging with headphones, everyone is Pascal's king.

The analysis of divertissement was central to Pascal's thought. It is not difficult to fathom why. Pascal was a Roman Catholic and defender of his faith. The *Pensées* is in fact an extended defense of the Christian religion, an apology. One of its aims is to expose the sources of unbelief, and for Pascal divertissement was among these. He was persuaded that only those who gaze within and conduct close self-examination, who seek stillness of body and silence of thought, can gain and preserve authentic religion. For Pascal, the God of Abraham, Isaac, and Jacob was to be found when human nature was at rest. The *logos* was to be heard in the silence, the divine fire beheld in the darkness.

Pascal's observation of a link between silence and religion is confirmed by a great cloud of witnesses. The entirety of the Christian tradition is here seconded by the rest of the world's sundry religions, which with one voice advise that faith without quiet is dead. The Koran and the Talmud, the Bible and the Avesta, the Darshanas and the Analects praise silence. Religions are at one in teaching that, without quiet, the roots of piety will at best be shallow. The idea that God speaks not with the wind or the earthquake or the fire but with a still, small voice is a commonplace; it is general religious wisdom. In all places and at all times those

longing to touch another world have instinctively known what to do —
enter a desert, climb a mountain, join a hermitage. "Be still, and know
that I am God."

One would do well to reflect upon the fact that God, the Holy One, is
silent. The Divinity does not speak to us as one person to another. Nor
does the air vibrate with sounds from a divine voice box. The situation is
indeed such that the Bible contains what the theologians call "special revelation." Its words on paper are the exception to the rule. For the rest, divine
communication is always indirect, always ambiguous, always a whisper.

Isaiah 45:15, one of Pascal's favorite verses, declares: "Truly, thou art a
God who hidest thyself." For those who do not believe, the elusiveness of
the Deity, God's apparent delight in the game of hide-and-seek, is a stum-
bling block, a cause for espousing deism (the Creator made us and went
away) or atheism (we made God and later found this out). But for those
of faith, the divine silence is a manifestation of uncircumscribed love.
"Love is long-suffering," or, as the King James Version has it, "Love
beareth all things, . . . endureth all things." And God endures in silence.
The whole creation groans and travails because the God of love refrains
from intruding in any obvious fashion, even when evil has run riot. As
Simone Weil puts it, "Love consents to all and commands only those who
consent. Love is abdication. God is abdication."

This fertile thought, which has roots in Origen and which has recently been developed so intriguingly by Geddes MacGregor, may be associated with the theme of the *imitatio Dei,* the imitation of God. Because the Supreme Being embodies all the virtues, to be virtuous is to be
like that Being. Plato wrote in the *Republic* that one becomes like God
through virtue, and Jesus is recorded as commanding, "Be merciful, even
as your Father is merciful" (Luke 6:36). The point for us is that silence is,
in the Christian tradition, a virtue, and it is embodied by God. Does this
not become for us an imperative — God's silence is our example?

The keeping of silence involves the imitation not only of the creator
but also of the creation. Cats meow, dogs bark, and birds sing; but such
sounds break nature's silence only intermittently. What percentage of a
lion's day is spent roaring? Like the stereotypical wise man, animals speak
only on occasion. Furthermore, they do not, from what we can divine,

restlessly yearn for din. To all appearances they contentedly pass their lives in the relative quiet of the great outdoors. Perhaps the myth that human beings long ago spoke the language of the animals should be taken to mean that once upon a time we spoke very little. "Go to the ant, O sluggard; consider her ways, and be wise" (Prov. 6:6).

Returning to the impact of science, or rather technology, on religion, the advance of the former and the retreat of the latter can take one more factor into account. Technology is like an ancient ruler with an extraordinarily large harem and an overcharged libido, to whom new sons and daughters are born every day, each adding one more cry. And, amid the other far-reaching changes that affect us in ways we never imagine, the stillness retreats. The upshot is that with our wills or without, at home or away, artificial sounds surround us. This can only reinforce whatever other impulses now push us toward what we call secularization.

It is not fanciful or romantic to observe that our planet was once a more quiet place, its common stillness broken only occasionally. Today, however, the occasional has become the unfailing. Sometimes inadvertently, but also often by design, technology's devices, unlike most of those designed by Nature's God, make commotion. The automobile, the dentist's drill, and the pinball machine — we would feel cheated if the pinball machine did not emit sounds — are quite unlike photosynthesis, the bounding cheetah, and passing clouds. These last are wonderfully quiet mechanisms. Again, a beaver fells trees with voiceless teeth, a lumberjack with deafening chain saws. Of course nature has its sounds, some of them quite loud: thunderclaps, volcanic eruptions, and earthquake rumbles. But these are punctuation marks, not sentences. In our modern world, on the other hand, sound is first, and those who wish to feel silence must often undertake an expedition.

We are so distant from the olden world that some enterprising persons now profit by selling tapes and videos that simply record the sounds of birds, leaves rustling in the wind, and waves striking the shore. Aldous Huxley penned these words in 1944:

The twentieth century is, among other things, the Age of Noise. Physical noise, mental noise, and noise of desire — we hold history's record for all of them. And no wonder; for all the resources of our almost miraculous technology have been thrown into the current assault against silence. That most popular and influential of all recent inventions, the radio, is nothing but a conduit through which prefabricated din can flow into our homes. And this din goes far deeper, of course, than the ear-drums. It penetrates the mind, filling it with a babel of distractions — news items, mutually irrelevant bits of information, blasts of corybantic or sentimental music, continually repeated doses of drama that bring no catharsis, but merely create a craving for daily or even hourly emotional enemas.

The state of affairs recounted by Huxley — worse now than then — should stir anxiety in anyone concerned for the future of religion. Our tradition teaches that confrontation with silence is requisite for the sincere religious pilgrim. Even Jesus, according to the Four Gospels, felt the need to go off by himself for prayer and contemplation. Arguing from the greater to the lesser, how much more should we? Our technology, however, has so populated the world with so many devices of distraction that it is now possible to spend the entire span of a human life without learning of silence. I know of a woman who cannot even *sleep* without the noise and light of her television.

This is no good omen. Anyone who pays heed to the Christian tradition — or to almost any religious tradition, for that matter — would have to wager that a significant increase in noise will make religion increasingly exotic, or at least radically change its nature and practices. One strongly suspects that the relatively unfrenzied atmosphere of most church services is partial cause for drops in attendance. How can those at ease with the frightful clamor and frenetic, disjointed images of MTV not be bored during a church service?

Perhaps Nietzsche was half-right. Maybe we have murdered God. But maybe the mortal wounds were inflicted by something other than our clever arguments. Perhaps we finally did away with God indirectly, by exterminating silence. Artificial noise has become an unholy liturgy that unites all in the aimless rush toward collective amnesia and banality, away from Nature's God and God's self-imposed muteness of love. As Jerome asked, "Where there is the beating of drums, the noise and clatter of pipe and lute, the clanging of cymbals, can any fear of God be found?"

Radio, as Huxley observed, is here the great parable, the outstanding lesson of what we covet. Which commandment is first of all? For those who give us radio, it is this: Let there be sound. Silence, the calamity labeled "dead air," must be entirely filled. And why? Not because there is an urgency to communicate vital facts. As G. K. Chesterton once observed, there is no necessary correlation between our ability to say much and our having anything much to say. Radio is the proof. Even assuming that so-called news broadcasts convey useful information, such broadcasts usually occupy only fragments of hours and at that are exceedingly repetitive. Radio's service clearly lies elsewhere. It ministers to us not by informing but by entertaining — that is, by distracting. It is there, a constant comrade, to muzzle silence. Like Muzak in shopping malls, its presupposition, its major premise, is that stillness is unwelcome, a thing to be avoided. It exists because people now so dislike quiet.

Who can doubt that radio's universal triumph is a symptom of a pervasive restlessness, or rather an ineffective placebo for the great *ennui* that has haunted the past two centuries? And who can dispute that the more we have fed our appetite for stimuli, the more ravenous we have become? Or is it more accurate to affirm that we have medicated our nervousness with things, such as noise, that make us more nervous?

Consumption in any case has functioned, as has advertising, to enlarge our felt lack. One is reminded of Ovid's King Erysichthon: *in epulis epulas quaerit:* In the midst of banquets he searched for a meal. It is altogether likely that numerous contemporary ills stem from the boredom engendered by the exhilaration of being Pascal's king. Excessive *divertissement* breeds dullness, and we have had *divertissement* to excess. Who among us is in real danger of meeting the once-dreaded Akedia, the noonday demon, the demon of weariness and monotony who so oppressed the cell-bound monks of earlier times? If Coleridge, in 1800, could rebuke his contemporaries for their "degrading thirst for outrageous stimulation," what would he make of us, who reserve our highest salaries for entertainers? We have, to be sure, some way to go before reaching the decadence of the upper-class Romans of the late Republic and early Empire. The specter of satiation and boredom that trailed their habitual revelry so haunted them that many alternated asceticism with indulgence — fasting or eating gruel in order to relish food, sleeping on boards to make their luxurious beds enjoyable, living in "paupers' huts," Epicurus explained, so as "to beguile the tedium of their lives." Seneca wrote of them, "Now it is a pleasure to be miserable." Perhaps that is the goal set before us.

However that may be, there is more to be said about the radio. The very air of the twenty-first century is different. Today, radio waves permeate all; they are our ether. If we only had eyes to see, we would perceive them everywhere. At this moment, in the palm of my hand, is all the information necessary to produce dozens of radio programs: it need only be translated by the right device. A radio can live anywhere, for its food is all about. As a result, even the seemingly quietest corner is potential noise, pregnant no longer with silence but with sound. And, by not thinking about this, we take the fact for granted, as though it were natural, which it is not. In the past the attribute of omnipresence was associated with God, not radio waves.

Radio is additionally problematic because it depreciates the word through inflation. An excess of anything leads to its devaluation, and we now have a superfluity of speech. How many words does a radio station cast abroad in a day? A week? A year? Can it really have so much to say? And what is taught by the prolixity? The lessons, all the better absorbed because never made explicit, are evident. Words are many and therefore cheap. They can be attended to halfheartedly and turned into something like background music. And, meaning little, they require no answer. But all this — which in part explains the immediate appeal of deconstructionism to many modern American college students — is idiocy. Words should be of inestimable value. They should hold our full attention. They should, as Augustine argued so strenuously, partake of or participate in the truth. And they should demand a response. This is why "on the day of judgment people will render account for every careless word they utter" (Matt. 12:36). If one were a radio, how would one fare at the great assize?

The addictive strength of noise was unforgettably demonstrated for me during graduate school, when I suffered the misfortune of living in an apartment whose thin floor was the ceiling for two female undergraduates. They had a vice that overcame my virtues. From waking moment to dream time, the radio, the television, or the stereo vomited noise, for my ears as well as theirs. There were even occasions on which the audio became visual, as when I saw my houseplants dance. Sane pleas for quiet went unheeded. Even the contingent notice of eviction I obtained from the landlord just turned the knobs down one notch. The most effective measure was my attempt, one Sunday morning at five A.M., to kick down their door. This endeavor, which I fortified with loud threats, gained some relief. This time the knobs were turned down two or three notches. But the unclean sounds were never fully exorcised, nor was my stolen silence ever given back. My neighbors were simply incapable of enduring stillness. For them it was a sort of torture, as their noise was to me; and they were as nonplussed by my desire for silence as I was by their unquenchable thirst for sound.

I am sure that the general tolerance for noise has increased in the last few decades, which have brought us cell phones and iPods. When Muzak first entered offices, regular periods of silence, of fifteen minutes' duration, were inserted into the musical stream, on the assumption that constant sound would beget irritability. Those periods of silence have since disappeared. It is also telling that commuters vigorously protested when Grand Central Station, in 1949, first piped in music and commercials. But their cause was lost, and nothing but incredulity would be the upshot if some group today made similar protest.

"Silence is golden." Sadly, the words sound archaic, like something one's great-grandmother might have said. We have here a dead proverb, or no proverb at all, if by that is meant a popular or oft-repeated byword. The same is true of these words from the Old Testament: "When words are many, transgression is not lacking, but the one who restrains his lips is prudent" (Prov. 10:19); "The one who belittles a neighbor lacks sense, but a person of understanding remains silent" (Prov. 11:12); "Prudent individuals conceal their knowledge, but fools proclaim their folly" (Prov. 12:23). Obviously we have lost the insight that silence begets wisdom. The image of a university student studying with headphones speaks worlds. Whereas, in the age of Wordsworth, "quiet as a nun" was a compliment, it would today be pejorative, a description of an introvert without self-esteem. Nor do we believe what Kierkegaard once observed, that "only someone who knows how to remain essentially silent can really talk."

Ironically, we were all wiser at a younger age. Children, we are told, learn more in the first year than in any other, maybe in all the other years put together. And that is the year in which they cannot speak. Infants do of course cry. But in the act of learning they are mostly silent. They look. They listen. They feel. And the words directed at them are received in silence, just as their decisions and innumerable experiments are carried out in the same. Should we not heed the words of Jesus and become again like little children?

Silence, let me emphasize at this juncture, should not be thought of as a negation, as the absence of sound. It should instead be envisaged as a desirable presence. Silence is the life-giving atmosphere human beings were intended to breathe, the heaven-sent manna that feeds soul, mind, and even body. It is, most importantly, the bridge between this plane of existence and whatever planes may lie beyond.

Max Picard, the French philosopher, wrote in his remarkable book *The World of Silence* that silence is "holy uselessness." His exposition merits review. Silence for Picard is "useless" because "it does not fit into the world of profit and utility; it simply *is*. It seems to have no other purpose;

it cannot be exploited. All the other great phenomena have been appropriated by the world of profit and utility," including earth, air, fire, and water; "even the space between heaven and earth has become a mere cavity for aeroplanes to travel through." But silence "stands outside the world of profit and utility; it cannot be exploited for profit; you cannot get anything out of it. It is 'unproductive.' Therefore it is regarded as valueless." Yet silence is, in truth, more useful than anything with "utility." It is indeed holy. For through its "power of autonomous being, silence points to a state where only being is valid: the state of the Divine. The mark of the Divine in things is preserved by their connection with the world of silence." Picard clarifies this point: "Silence is a basic phenomenon. That is to say, it is a primary, objective reality, which cannot be traced back to anything else. It cannot be replaced by anything else; it cannot be exchanged with anything else. There is nothing behind it to which it can be related except the Creator Himself." Silence is sacred. It cannot be made secular.

There is ancient historical precedent for Picard's ruminations. In a Jewish liturgy preserved among the Dead Sea Scrolls, memorable expression is given to the conviction that silence is not a vacuum waiting to be filled but instead a substantial and sacred reality that is wrapped around the Creator. In the "Songs of the Sabbath Sacrifice," which unfortunately survives only in pieces, we read in one place, "The cherubim fall before Him and bless. As they rise, the sound of divine stillness [is heard], and there is a tumult of jubilation as their wings lift up, the sound of divine [stillnes]s." In another place there is this: "From underneath the wondrous sanctuary (comes) the sound of quiet stillness, the heavenly beings bless . . . the king. . . ." The intentionally paradoxical phrases "the sound of divine stillness" and "the sound of quiet stillness" are provocative. When the cherubim praise God, the sound they make is inaudible. In other words, God is praised by mute mouths. The idea, this silence of the angels, which no doubt reflects the conviction that the Holy One can never be contained in our language, is compelling.

Interestingly enough, it found its way into the Christian tradition. We find this in Pseudo-Dionysius: "The angel is an image of God, a manifestation of the invisible light, a burnished mirror, bright, untarnished, without spot or blemish, receiving, if it is reverent to say, all the beauty of the absolute divine goodness, and, so far as is possible, *kindling in itself, with perfect radiance, the goodness of the secret silence."* Compare with this the beautiful hymn of Ephrem the Syrian: "Thousands of thousands stand, and tens of thousands haste. The thousands and ten thousands cannot search out the One: for all of them stand in silence and serve. He has no heir of his throne, save the Son who is of Him. In the midst of silence is the enquiry into Him. When the angels come and search Him out, they attain to silence and are stayed." Another old Syrian teacher, Abraham of Nathpar, stated that prayer without the voice makes one like the angels Gabriel and Michael, who sing their "holy" without any words. Much closer to our own time are the lines from the poem of the American Quaker John Greenleaf Whittier:

> With silence only as their benediction
> God's angels come
> Where, in the shadow of a great affliction,
> The soul sits dumb.

I should like to suggest that we make our own the ancient tradition of still heavenly hosts. That angels are voiceless means that God is ringed in silence. But this silence carries jubilation and thanksgiving. "To Thee, silence is praise," as it says in an old Jewish commentary on the Psalms. Heaven's stillness is not empty but full. One is reminded of the words of Isaac of Nineveh: silence is "the language of the kingdom of heaven." The same thought was given expression by St. John of the Cross when he wrote, "The Father uttered one Word; that Word is His Son, and He utters Him for ever in everlasting silence; and in silence the soul has to hear it."

Already at the beginning of the second century, in Ignatius of Antioch, we read that God's Word, Jesus Christ, "proceeded from silence," and that the one who "truly possesses the word of Jesus is able also to hearken unto his silence."

Silence is not nothing. It is instead the divine liturgy leading to communion with God, the mute awe and reverence required by encounter with the holy. I am reminded of the legend in an old apocryphal gospel. When the Virgin Mary conceived, when God became a human being,

> a great silence descended with a great fear. For even the winds stopped, they made no breezes. There was no motion of tree leaves, nor sound of water. The streams did not flow, there was no motion of the sea. All things in the ocean were silent, and no human voice was heard. . . . Time almost stopped its measure. All, overwhelmed with great fear, kept silent.

As with the advent of God in the world, so too with the advent of God in our lives: silence is the only appropriate greeting.

Beyond the noise of this world is the divine stillness of another, a stillness in which one may find "the Father who is in secret." And yet we typically pass our waking hours alert for every random murmur. Philo of Alexandria says somewhere: "Understanding is starved when the senses feast, as on the other side it makes merry when they are fasting." Our faith demands that we enable the ears of the soul to listen for what the poet Rilke calls "the uninterrupted news that grows out of the silence." "Be silent, all flesh, before the LORD" (Zech. 2:13).

John Climacus, in his *Ladder of Divine Ascent,* wrote, "Intelligent silence is the mother of prayer, freedom from bondage, custodian of zeal, a guard on our thoughts, a watch on our enemies . . . a companion of stillness, the opponent of dogmatics, a growth of knowledge, a hand to shape contemplation, hidden progress, the secret journey upward." These words are from another world. Few any longer feel, few really believe, that silence merits such high praise, that it is, as a certain rabbi once said, "a medicine for everything." Who now concurs with *The Sayings of Syriac Menader* (an old collection of proverbs) that "there exists nothing better than silence"? Our culture is fettered to the five senses, engrossed in distractions. But all reason and experience insist that the wise wriggle out of the ever-enlarging abyss of noise that constantly whirls all about, directionless. "Listen to me in silence, O coastlands" (Isa. 41:1). If humanity's destiny is, as Jesus once said, to be like the angels in heaven, then perhaps there is even now an imperative to keep the angelic quiet, to fashion earplugs against the modern sirens of sound, to construct our own Faraday cages, boxes where noise cannot reach. Nature has given us eyelids but not earlids, so we must make them for ourselves.

I end by recording the desire of an anonymous Syrian monk who, fourteen centuries ago, in a world much quieter than ours, offered this prayer: "Grant, O Lord, by your grace, that my mind may converse with the greatness of that grace — not with a language produced by the body's voice or uttered by the tongue of flesh, but grant rather that converse which praises you in silence, you the Silent One."

CHAPTER 2

The Luminous Dusk

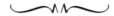

I see black light.

The dying words of Victor Hugo

The night will not be taken by storm, conquered by lights. So treated, it retreats and remains alien, threatening just beyond the circle of light cast by the lantern, full of fearful shapes and ominous shadows. Encroaching upon it with our lights, we cannot come to know it.

Erazim Kohák

O Compassion and Mercy, who have been sent into the world, O Hope of creation, cause me to taste of the delight of your hope, so that I may be blind as far as the world is concerned but be illumined in spirit.

Isaac of Nineveh

One mid-afternoon, when I was twenty-four years old, I walked by my apartment window, which framed a garden in the cemetery next door. I noticed that the scene, which I had looked at often enough to pay no more attention, was somehow magically transfigured. Everything was self-shining as my eyes saw not the surface of things but through them. The trees and tulips were colored jewels, the air a clear crystal, the boulders (in the words of Ezekiel) stones of fire. The whole multicolored bliss was a sea of glass, each object a stained-glass window. A preternatural brilliance, a slowly breathing radiance, intense yet painless, the essence of beauty, suffused everything; and a thought arose in my mind: the expulsion from Eden was only a dimming of vision; we are even yet in paradise.

The experience, although unique in my life, is evidently common enough. Surely Plato's description in the *Phaedo* of the colors of "the real earth" (a description that includes the remark that "the colors which we know are only limited samples") reflects the same experience. So too the famous opening lines of Wordsworth's *Intimations,* where we read of meadow, grove, and stream, the earth, and every common sight "apparelled in celestial light." There are also numerous parallels in the archives of the Religious Experience Research Centre at the University of Wales, Lampeter. Consider the following experience of a child alone on a moor:

> An indescribable peace, which I have since tried to describe as a "diamond moment of reality," came flowing into (or indeed, waking up within) me, and I realized that all around me everything was lit with a kind of inner shining beauty — the rocks, bracken, bramble bushes, view, sky and even blackberries — and also myself. . . . And in that moment, sweeping in on that tide of light, there came also knowledge. The knowledge that though disaster was moving slowly and seemingly unavoidably towards me (and this I had known subconsciously for some time) yet in the end "All would be well."

The most compelling account of this sort of experience I have happened across appears in *The Candle of Vision,* the very strange book published under the initials AE (the sometime pen name of George William Russell). Indeed, at one point the narrative so accurately describes what I saw and thought that a literary critic might wrongly suspect my own story of being merely a literary doublet: "The winds were sparkling and diamond clear, and yet full of color as an opal, as they glittered through the valley, and I knew the Golden Age was all about me, and it was we who had been blind to it, but that it had never passed away from the world."

The controversial Hesychasts, Byzantine mystics, taught the possibility of seeing the divine light with corporeal eyes; and I have wondered whether my experience was akin to theirs. Perhaps it is presumptuous to suppose so, and maybe I have confused nature mysticism with supernatural mysticism. I recall that the light seen by Simeon the New Theologian, who so strongly influenced Hesychasm, was unlike mine in that it came from above and made the world disappear. Further, my experience was not preceded by fasting, meditation, or a life of sanctity. Just maybe, however, the divine grace occasionally enjoys opening the eyes of the undeserving. However that may be, I shall not forget the luminous cemetery garden; and I have no reason to regard as peculiar the notion that all of Nature is bathed in a subtle divine energy.

That notion has been part of Christian theology. T. S. Eliot wrote, "Light, light . . . visible reminder of the invisible light." This line draws upon an old Christian tradition, one of Platonic stock. There is the created light of day that comes from the stars. But this physical light is only a sign, the material underside of the uncreated light of Christ, the eternal light beheld at the Transfiguration by three men whose eyes for a moment shed their scales. (As Eastern Christian tradition teaches, it was not Jesus, the ever-luminous, who changed, but his disciples, who were otherwise ever-blind.) This is the nimbus or angelic light that appears in stories — not all of them legends — about St. Francis of Assisi, Seraphim of Sarov, and so many other saints. It is the light of the New Jerusalem, which has no need of sun or moon to shine upon it, for the glory of God is its light, and its lamp is the Lamb. It is this supernatural light that the Hesychast mystics of Byzantium longed to behold, and not just in the world to come. As Boethius wrote of his own experience, "He who once has seen this light, will not call the sunbeam bright."

While we cannot know to what extent religious experiences of light (however interpreted) have contributed to the circumstance, the religions of the world have unanimously associated light with the divine. The Indo-European word for the chief deity, *dyeu-poder* (from whence come the Greek "Zeus Pater" and the Latin "Jupiter"), derives from two roots, the first meaning "to shine." The Pharaoh Akhenaton identified the sole God with the sun disk. According to Buddhist texts, when Siddhartha Gautama, sitting under a fig tree, gained enlightenment, the highest heaven exploded with light. Light stands for salvation already in the Code of Hammurabi, and old Iranian religion taught that the divine part of the soul is light, while Jewish tradition taught that both the bodies of angels and the garments of resurrected saints are luminous.

In our Christian tradition, Jesus Christ is the light of the world, while Christians are "children of the light" who are called to "walk in the light": "Awake, O sleeper, and arise from the dead, and Christ shall give you light" (Eph. 5:14). God, whose first creative act was, according to Genesis, the letting go of light, and who inaugurated the Exodus from Egypt by appearing in a burning bush, is light and "the Father of lights," "and in him is no darkness at all." Protestants sing that God lives "in light inaccessible hid from our eyes," and "only the splendor of light hideth Thee."

The prominence of light in religious texts and theology is matched by its prominence in religious ritual. One thinks of the worship of fire among the Parsis, of the seven-branched menorah of Judaism, of the eternal fire nurtured by the Roman Vestal Virgins, of the dramatic candle service that opens the Eastern Orthodox Pascha. The Protestant ban on the ceremonial use of candles, born of opposition to perceived Roman Catholic superstition, is an anomaly in the history of religions. It is the exception to the rule that everywhere religion has made use of fire. It is no surprise that time has seen most Protestant groups restore at least a few candles.

Our natural love of light, so manifest in sacred texts and rituals, has perhaps shown itself pre-eminently in the evolution of the Western city. During the Middle Ages towns went dark at sundown. Then gates were shut, doors to private dwellings were locked, and a curfew fell. Only night watchmen with torches and citizens with torches — and good excuses — were permitted to walk the streets: "And no man walke after IX of the belle streken in the nyght withoute lyght or without cause reasonable in payne of empresonment" (English decree, 1467). But urban darkness began to draw back in the sixteenth century, when laws required all houses to display lights at night, and then again in the seventeenth century, when public lanterns were, for the first time, fixed on street posts — as in pre-Revolutionary Paris, which had several thousand such lanterns. (We know this from the history books because the rebellious citizens had such a grand time smashing them.)

In the nineteenth century, gaslights, which greatly decreased crime in London, replaced the old oil lamps, after which arc lighting replaced gaslights, with the result that streets became truly well-lit for the first time. It was then that light from one artificial source reached the light of the next, so that the glow of individual orbs merged to produce something akin to daylight. Indeed, some cities, especially in North America, were so enthralled by the new possibilities that they installed what was known as tower lighting. While Napoleon declined to fill Paris with "lighthouses," the authorities in Detroit built 122 towers, each approximately 150 feet high, each holding aloft extremely bright arc lights. The purpose was to illuminate the entire city. While the method proved to be a short-lived utopian fantasy, inefficient and expensive, our modern cities, with their novel nightlife, are now brightly lit. Not only do the streetlights create illumined labyrinths, but often tall buildings are, like Christmas trees, covered with decorative lights. The progress of civilization is the multiplication of lights.

Clearly, light is something we crave. We love bonfires, fireworks, and the radiance of advertising signs. We constantly banish the shadows. How many matches have been struck since the advent of safe phosphorous in the 1830s? It is peculiar that Mother Nature equipped only fireflies with luminescence to call for intercourse (for that is why they light up): it

would have worked with humans too. Certainly vendors have successfully attracted buyers by doing nothing more than aiming spotlights at
the sky; and how many times has the big screen hypnotized us with the
lights of Las Vegas? We are like bugs at the porch light.

To return to religion: because darkness and light are antithetical, the one
the vanquisher of the other, the goodness of light has, as everyone
knows, its correlate in the badness of darkness. For every text about light
and life there is another about darkness and death. Paul wrote of "sense-
less minds" being "darkened," of "works of darkness," of "powers of
darkness," and of "things of darkness." He also told his Christian readers
that they, because of the salvation wrought for them by Jesus Christ,
were no longer "in darkness." Proverbs 4:19 says that "the way of the
wicked is like deep darkness," and Ecclesiastes 2:14 declares that "the fool
walks in darkness."

Throughout the world's religions darkness is indeed the outstanding
symbol of evil. In classical Zoroastrianism, for instance, the good creator
Ohrmazd is all light, the evil destroyer Ahrman all darkness. In the
Bhagavad Gita of Hinduism, darkness *(tamas),* one of the three fundamental components of human nature, stifles wisdom, engenders ignorance, and produces sloth. In the Dead Sea Scrolls, the reprobate are the
"sons of darkness," they walk in "all the ways of darkness," and their
leader is "the angel of darkness." In Neoplatonism, as in early
Gnosticism, the human soul is in difficulty because it has fallen from the
region of light above to the darkness of matter below. And, to return to
Christianity, hell, which in the Gospel of Matthew is referred to as "the
outermost darkness," is, despite its fire, an area where, to quote Dante,
"no light shines." The frightful destination is underground because there
it is dark. Lactantius, the early Christian apologist, could write, "The
Lord so divided the world with the Devil that the West, the North, *the
darkness,* and the cold fell to the sphere of the adversary." Although "Lucifer" literally means "the shining one," he is known as "the prince of
darkness"; and prior to late medieval art, which colors him red (after the

fires of hell), the devil is always brown or gray, or, as in the Epistle of Barnabas and Athanasius's *Life of Anthony*, black.

It goes without saying that the use of darkness as a symbol for evil is not special to religion. From Homer's *Odyssey*, in which the kingdom of the dead is under the curtain of "dreadful night," to Joseph Conrad's *Heart of Darkness* and Elie Wiesel's *Night*, darkness is a stock item. In world mythology, fairy tales, poetry, and stories of every kind, it is everywhere the companion of evil. Tolkien's "Dark Lord" sends forth nine black riders. In Slavonic tradition the vampire is the soul of a suicide or heretic or other sinful person that comes forth only at night, for it cannot endure the light of day. Again, Lady Macbeth, when she determines to have King Duncan murdered, speaks thus: "Come, thick night, / And pall thee in the dunnest smoke of hell, / That my keen knife see not the wound it makes, / Nor heaven peep through the blanket of the dark, / To cry, 'Hold, Hold!'" Passages such as this, in which darkness is the soil of sin, are ubiquitous. If anything belongs to the collective unconscious postulated by Jung, it must be darkness, for its negative connotations are much the same everywhere.

Why are the unpleasant associations of darkness so fixed in the human mind? There are at least four indisputable reasons, the first being that darkness is the antithesis of light, and light is universally reckoned a good thing. Light brings warmth and activates sight, our most important sense. It further sustains all life, for it is the energy of plants, which are the base of our food chain. It follows that darkness, whose relationship to light is like that of evil to good (that is, the one is nothing, simply the negation or absence of the other), must make things cold, render animals blind, and turn the living into the dead. Certainly this is what the fascinating black hole of modern cosmology does: it sucks and swirls everything into nothingness. One remembers in this connection Lord Byron's poem "Darkness," which gruesomely recounts the end of the world. It opens with this:

> I had a dream, which was not all a dream.
> The bright sun was extinguished, and the stars
> Did wander darkling in the eternal space,
> Rayless, and pathless, and the icy earth

Swung blind and blackening in the moonless air;
Morn came and went — and came, and brought no day,
And men forgot their passions in the dread
Of this their desolation; and all hearts
Were chilled into a selfish prayer for light.

The poem ends in this fashion:

    The world was void,
The populous and the powerful was a lump
Seasonless, herbless, treeless, manless, lifeless —
A lump of death — a chaos of hard clay.
The rivers, lakes, and ocean all stood still,
And nothing stirred within their silent depths;
Ships sailorless lay rotting on the sea,
And their masts fell down piecemeal: as they dropped
They slept on the abyss without a surge —
The waves were dead; the tides were in their grave,
The Moon, their mistress, had expired before;
The winds were withered in the stagnant air,
And the clouds perished; Darkness had no need
Of aid from them — She was the Universe.

Already in the Gospel of Mark we read that, at the world's end, "the sun shall be darkened and the moon will not give its light, and the stars will be falling down from heaven." This cosmic darkness, which marks history's end, also appears in stories about the deaths of famous individuals, including Adam, Romulus, Julius Caesar, and Jesus. How can darkness not be evil?

The link, remarked above, between darkness and blindness is a second cause for linking darkness to evil. According to Genesis 1:2, "The earth was without form and void, and darkness was upon the face of the deep." The proposition that "there was a time when all was darkness" (Berossus) is also found in Babylonian, Phoenician, Greek, African, and Native American creation myths.

This might have been anticipated. Darkness — the milieu of our confused nightmares — means invisibility, and this in turn means a lack of separation and distinction; and that in turn means disorder. Creation, on the other hand, entails coherence, stability, hierarchy, things that can be perceived only when darkness is banished, when there is light, for light shows up differences.

Sight, accordingly, is understanding, and "enlightenment" means "to be free from ignorance." To be in darkness, on the other hand, is to fail to comprehend. This is why, in Plato's *Republic,* those without true knowledge are represented by chained individuals who sit in a dark cave and behold only shadows on the wall, shadows cast by a fire they cannot see, and why the "Dark Ages" are (quite erroneously) called what they are called. Death, the great unknown, has frequently been thought of as darkness. In the *Epic of Gilgamesh,* it is the house "bereft of light." In the *Iliad* we read, "Death is near, and black." And Tennyson wrote, "Twilight and evening bell, / And after that the dark." Bacon wrote to similar effect: "Men fear death as children fear to go into the dark." Job put it most memorably: "Are not the days of my life few? Let me alone, that I may find a little comfort before I go whence I shall not return, to the land of gloom and deep darkness, the land of gloom and chaos, where light is as darkness" (10:20-22). Death is, to use an old phrase, a "leap into the dark." That mortuaries always dim lights when a body is on view may be interpreted as a profound symbol. Certainly the darkness of the tomb is fitting.

Children, as Bacon's words remind, are afraid of the dark. Why? The answer is simple: because they know not what it holds. Turn on the lights and all is well. Sight brings knowledge, and knowledge is assurance. It is the same with adults. If a child's parents are unafraid of the bedroom's dark, it is only because their minds are unaffected — that is, they know, from memory, where things are, and also that, on that score, darkness makes no difference. But put the parents in an unknown place and withhold all light, and they will be as apprehensive as the child. Blindness is ignorance, and ignorance is fear.

To this one may add that we cannot read in the dark, nor do we often choose to converse without light. It follows that learning, whose foundation is the lecture and books, must, at least subconsciously, be linked with light, and that darkness, by implication, cannot be educational. Again, then, darkness equals ignorance.

A third reason darkness everywhere dons the robe of evil is that human groups have moral standards. To recall C. S. Lewis's *The Abolition of Man*, all societies, notwithstanding their many differences, have acknowledged the Tao, the principle that certain things are right, and certain things wrong. But because, as Paul knew so well, ours is a fallen world with sinful citizens, the Tao is often broken. The point to make is that conscious transgression of the Tao frequently takes place beneath darkness, where disapproving eyes cannot probe. Vandals destroy property at night and burglars prowl after the sun has gone down in order to escape detection. Adulterers hurry into dark rooms in out-of-the-way places and pull down the blinds. For them, as Clement of Alexandria wrote, "darkness is a veil to conceal their passion." One understands why prostitutes are known as "ladies of the evening," and why houses of ill repute belong to what are called "red-light districts." Those engaged in illicit sexual activity are customarily creatures of the night, and when light is absolutely necessary, they favor something other than the full spectrum.

A fourth factor bestowing upon darkness its evil reputation is of course experience of the weather. Foul weather is always associated with clouds, and clouds obscure the light. Tornadoes strike and floods fall, hail crashes and thunder claps when the sky grows dark. All this cannot but have a profound effect upon humanity's psyche. Darkness is a harbinger of trouble in our thoughts because it is a harbinger of trouble in the world at large.

Having ventured that there are at least four causes for the constant conjoining of darkness and evil, I should like to suggest that there may also be a fifth. In his *Confessions*, Augustine writes that, after the death of a childhood friend, his despondency was marked by a heart "black with grief." We understand the expression. For us too the thought of depression inevitably conjures up a gray and murky darkness. Presumably this is the case in part because physical darkness stimulates the production of melatonin, a hormone seemingly connected with melancholy — a fact thought by some to explain why the shorter, light-deprived days of winter beget in many what is called Seasonal Affective Disorder. Withdrawal of the sun breeds sadness.

But it is even more notable that those stricken by a psychological darkness within are driven to seek a corresponding physical darkness without. It is not just that those in mourning traditionally wear black. Still more striking is the circumstance that people who are severely depressed tend to distance themselves from bright lights. The explanation for this I do not know. But it is also the case that such people typically have the habit of drooping their heads and keeping their eyes less than fully open, as though to shut out as much light as possible. The outstanding example is grieving widows, who traditionally wear black veils. Once more the biological or, more precisely, chemical explanation — there must be one — is not known to me. This does not, however, in any way alter the behavioral fact: depression cultivates darkness.

I have mentioned both the Transfiguration of Jesus and his passion in darkness. It is remarkable how the two events, as recounted in the first three Gospels, present themselves as antitheses and wage a symbolic battle of light against darkness.

In Matthew 17:1-8, Jesus takes Peter, James, and John to a high mountain where heaven comes to earth: Jesus' face shines as the sun, his garments become white as light, Moses and Elijah appear, a voice from a shining cloud speaks ("This is my beloved Son, with whom I am well pleased; listen to him"), and the disciples fall on their faces and fear exceedingly.

There is one other place in Matthew where people fear exceedingly: after the centurion and those with him see the miraculous signs attendant upon the Crucifixion. The link is small, but it prods one to observe that also common to the Transfiguration and the Crucifixion are the confession of Jesus as God's "Son" (17:5; 27:54), the presence of three named onlookers (in 17:1, three male disciples: Peter, James, and John; in 27:55-56, three female disciples: Mary Magdalene, Mary of James and Joseph, and the mother of the sons of Zebedee), and the number six ("after six days," 17:1; "from the sixth hour," 27:45).

Furthermore, these shared features exist in the midst of dramatic contrasts:

Transfiguration, 17:1-8	Crucifixion, chapter 27
Jesus takes others (1)	Jesus is taken by others (31)
elevation on mountain (1)	elevation on cross (35)
private epiphany (1)	public spectacle (39-40)
light (2)	darkness (45)
garments illumined (2)	garments stripped off (28, 35)
Jesus is glorified (2ff.)	Jesus is shamed (27ff.)
Elijah appears (3)	Elijah does not appear (45-50)
two saints beside Jesus (3)	two criminals beside Jesus (38)
God confesses Jesus (5)	God abandons Jesus (46)
reverent prostration (6)	mocking prostration (29)

Between Matthew 17:1-8 and Matthew 27:27-56 there is a curious confluence of similar motifs and contrasting images. We have here, whether intended by the author or not, pictorial antithetical parallelism, something like a diptych in which the two plates have similar outlines but different colors. If one scene were sketched on a transparency and placed over the other, many of its lines would disappear.

Despite their similarities, the two Gospel scenes represent the extremities of human experience. One tells of spit and mockery, nails and nakedness, blood and loneliness, torture and death. The other makes visible the presence of God and depicts the divinization of human nature. Moreover, the contradiction of experience, the coincidence of opposites in one person, is forcefully felt in the colors: the triumph is white, and the tragedy is black. It is the same old story: darkness encompasses misery; light reveals glory.

And yet we find the saving event not on Tabor but on Calvary. Why? Notwithstanding the darkness of hell, the lights of our cities, and the wearing of veils, the symbolic associations of light and darkness are not invariable. We may pay electrical companies huge sums to illumine our houses after dark, and we may reserve the darkness of solitary confinement for our most unrepentant lawbreakers, but these facts do not close the book. When Prometheus, against the will of Zeus, brought down fire from heaven, he was bound in chains, and those who received the heavenly light were punished by the coming of Pandora. Perhaps light has its costs.

Some have certainly thought so, and the artificial lighting of our world has not been hailed with universal enthusiasm. Many have at least thought too much artificial light undesirable. Robert Louis Stevenson wrote his famous essay "A Plea for Gas Lamps" because he found the dim light of gas, which he felt gave "a warm domestic radiance fit to eat by," more congenial than the harsh, bright light of electricity, which he deemed "horrible, unearthly, obnoxious." Again, Jules Michelet, in 1845, complained of the new use of artificial night lights in factories:

> These newly built big halls, flooded by brilliant light, torture eyes accustomed to darker quarters. Here there is no darkness, into which thought can withdraw, here there are no shadowy corners in which the imagination can indulge its dreams. No illusion is possible in this light. Incessantly and mercilessly, it brings us back to reality.

It is perhaps not surprising that the proliferation of household lamps and their growing efficiency throughout the nineteenth century effected not only the advent of curtains for the common home but also the progressive darkening and thickening of lampshades (culminating in the Tiffany). By the end of the century, the prospect of an ever-lighted night, desired by so many, was thought by some to be a dreaded nightmare.

In *When the Sleeper Wakes* (1899), H. G. Wells wrote of an authoritarian state that covered the sky with giant cantilevers and a translucent sheet, so that "gigantic globs of cool white light shamed the pale sunbeams that filtered down through the girders and wires." Nearer our time, the German art historian Wilhelm Hausenstein, after spending many hours in underground candlelight while Allied bombers passed overhead, judged that in electric light objects seem to "appear much more clearly" but in reality are "flattened." Such light "imparts too much brightness," whereas in candlelight "objects cast much more significant shadows" and "retain their poetic element."

This preference for less light has an arresting parallel in one man's religious experience. In *The Secret Gospel of Mark,* the account of his discovery of a controversial ancient document, the late Morton Smith, eminent scholar of antiquity at Columbia University, told of his several visits, during the 1940s and 1950s, to an old Eastern Orthodox church in Palestine, Mar Saba. During liturgy, the cloudy, flickering candles, the haunting icons, the pungent incense, and the unfamiliar chanting transported Smith to another world, and he, though not sharing the monks' faith, found it all strangely attractive:

> The painted walls reflected the dim light as if it came from a remote distance, and in the vast, vaguely luminous space thus created the huge black frescoes of the saints and monks of old stood like solid presences all around, the great figures of the eternal and universal Church, present in this realm among the stars, above space and time, the unchanging kingdom of the heavens, where the eternal service was offered to God.

Sometime between his visits, however, the monks removed the candles. In their place they put electric lights. For Smith the magic was gone. With the harsh, steady, cold light of electricity, the mystery was dispelled. Unbelief was no longer shadowed by doubt. Bright light quashed all feelings of the transcendent. I remember a line from Shelley:

> When the cloud is scattered
> The rainbow's glory is dead.

What does one make of Smith's experience? Whether or not churches should light wax or switch on current — a dead issue which should perhaps not be dead — the Supreme Being can certainly come to us whether our pupils are constricted or open full. Worship does not require disorientation.

Yet that is not the end of the matter, for the Bible itself speaks of God dwelling in thick darkness. In Exodus 20:21, we read that "the people stood afar off [from Mount Sinai], while Moses drew near to the thick darkness where God was." In 2 Samuel 22 there is a hymn of David that includes these lines: "He bowed the heavens, and came down; thick darkness was under his feet. He rode on a cherub, and flew; he was seen upon the wings of the wind. He made darkness around him his canopy . . ." (vv. 10-12). Almost exactly the same words appear in Psalm 18:11. And then there is 1 Kings 8:12, where the wise Solomon declares, "The LORD has set the sun in the heavens, but has said that he would dwell in thick darkness."

Why does darkness surround God in the Scriptures? The first and most obvious reason is that God is a mystery. The Divinity is transcendent, wholly other. So we are necessarily in ignorance and see through a glass darkly. The Cappadocian Father Gregory of Nyssa observed that when Moses climbed Sinai, he began in the daylight at the foot of the mountain, then moved up into the clouds, and finally met God at the top, in darkness. In this progression into night, Gregory divined a parable of the Christian life: "The true vision and the true knowledge of what we seek consists precisely in not seeing, in an awareness that our goal transcends all knowledge and is everywhere cut off from us by the darkness of incomprehensibility."

Beyond the natural association of darkness with things mysterious, there is the peculiar circumstance that physical light has the property of invisibility. It cannot be seen, and yet it illumines all about: the unperceived makes perception possible. One can fabricate an empty box whose interior surfaces are unilluminated when a light beam is projected into it — in which case a glance through the viewport reveals nothing but the blackness of empty space. Light itself is a sort of blank, a strange darkness.

This is one reason its general nature has been the subject of so much discussion, why Newton and Euler and Maxwell and the quantum physicists have all had different ideas. Is light corpuscular? Or an undulation in the ether? Or an electromagnetic vibration? Or is it a form of energy conveyed through empty space, an energy that in some circumstances seems to be a particle, in other circumstances a wave? This last is today's theory; but it produces puzzlement, and surely the future will see some other conjecture. Light hides itself. Its essence remains unknown. And if it is not reflected or refracted, it altogether disappears, as though nonexistent. (Photons, we are told, actually have no mass and no charge.) The analogy with God, who is eternally hidden and known only through effects, was worked out long ago by Augustine and other church fathers. Here, however, I wish to pursue another line of thought, to consider not the theology of darkness but a psychological point.

Both the physical and the mental planes of existence are on fire with interesting stimuli inviting response. Some require attention; some do not. But only one thing is truly needful, and that is God. It is our fallen fate, however, to heed innumerable trivialities, to turn our heads toward every passing light. We are stimuli-seeking machines. The unhappy circumstance is such that it requires informed and sustained effort to ignore juvenile distractions and to enter that solitary state in which the ever-present One comes to be known as present, in which the One who always knocks at the doors of hearts can be heard.

The way to achieve this, as we instinctively know, is to dampen the senses and quiet thoughts, treating everything as a diversion to be avoided. "Let us cast aside all earthly care," as the liturgy of Chrysostom has it. For this reason the religiously inclined attend church and aspire to enter another sort of space and time. Or they make a retreat, to focus otherwise scattered attention. Or, in the words of Matthew 6, they enter a closet and pray. Or they simply close their eyes.

For most of us in the West, prayer is almost automatically accompanied by closed eyes, because otherwise thoughts inevitably wander to whatever the physical light happens upon. This is reason to love the dark. Cyril, the fourth-century bishop of Jerusalem, understood this when he wrote,

> When does our mind tend more towards psalmody and prayer? Is this not at night? When do we come oftener to the remembrance of

our own sins? Is it not at night? Therefore let us not perversely entertain the thought that God is not the author of darkness, for experience shows that this too is good and most useful.

These words require special attention at this point in history, for the ongoing multiplication of lights means that most of us spend less and less
time in darkness.

But it is not just literal, external darkness that the pilgrim should happily enter. There must also be an inner darkness, an unlighted chamber
within. Although we should find God in the natural world around us,
and while we are commanded to find God in the neighbor next to us,
there is also an imperative for a turning to the Divine that requires a turning from the world, what Evelyn Underhill calls "a deliberate drawing-in
from the circumference to the centre." Here I follow Meister Eckhart,
who once interpreted darkness as "a silence and a stillness apart from the
commotion of creatures." Before there is a Presence, there must be an
absence.

Evagrius Ponticus, the fourth-century Origenist monk, asserted in
one fascinating chapter of his manual on prayer that demons "stimulate a
specific site in the brain," that is, "agitate the cerebral circulation" in order to make the soul at prayer see a light and so become disturbed. For
Evagrius, demons did not extinguish light but shed it. Perhaps he had in
mind Paul's remark about Satan disguising himself as an angel of light,
or the incident in Athanasius's *Life of Anthony* in which a demon wears
light. However that may be, the soul seeking God must enter the cloud
of unknowing; it must, as the Buddha said in his Fire Sermon, look beyond the eye and eye-consciousness; it must, as Dante Gabriel Rossetti
wrote in "Silent Noon," find an inner sanctuary filled with "visible silence, still as the hourglass." We were physically formed in the darkness
of the womb, and we are spiritually formed in the darkness of our minds.
As in the creation story, so too in each individual life: darkness comes before light.

Pascal was converted when he saw the fire of the God of Abraham, Isaac, and Jacob from about half past ten in the evening until half past midnight, when it was black. St. Francis, plagued with poor eyesight, received his stigmata when he saw a crucified Seraph descend from heaven "some time before dawn." And the Apostle Paul, so Acts tells us, became a Christian by going blind: "and when his eyes were opened, he could see nothing" (9:8). Blindness is the precondition of spiritual perception. As the Scripture says, "If your eye causes you to sin, pluck it out and throw it away" (Matt. 18:9). Just as it is sinners who are justified, so is it the sightless who see.

The Messiah first entered our world, as the Christmas hymn has it, in "silent night, holy night," and likewise does he come now, in what the German poet Novalis calls "the heavenly approach of night." This means that those who seek the Light of the World must first leave this world's light, after which the mind's own lights must likewise be abandoned. Perhaps this is what the inscrutable Chinese philosopher Lao-tzu had in mind when he spoke of "darkness within darkness, the gateway to all understanding." In any case, I find it fitting that Roman Christianity once thrived in the darkness of the catacombs.

"I am the God who made the light and created the darkness." These words from Isaiah are an invitation to enter the shadows, in the hope of discovering what Cyril called "that night whose darkness is daylight." The fourteenth-century Greek theologian Gregory Palamas, defender of Hesychism, wrote,

> After the cessation of perceiving and thinking, accomplished not only in words but in reality, there remains an unknowing which is beyond knowledge; though indeed a darkness, it is yet beyond radiance, and, as the great Denys says, it is in this dazzling darkness that the divine things are given to the saints.

God hides in the darkness, so to the darkness we must go.

I close by quoting the Welsh metaphysical poet Henry Vaughan. His poem "The Night," whose headnote is John 3:2 (Nicodemus "came to Jesus by night"), ends with these words:

Were all my loud, evil days
Calm and unhaunted as is thy dark tent,
Whose peace but by some angel's wing or voice
    Is seldom rent;
  Then I in Heaven all the long year
  Would keep and never wander here.

  But living where the sun
Doth all things wake, and where all mix and tire
Themselves and others, I consent and run
    To every mire,
  And by this world's ill-guiding light,
  Err more than I can do by night.

  There is in God, some say,
A deep, but dazzling darkness; as men here
Say it is late and dusky, because they
    See not all clear.
  O for that night! where I in Him
  Might live invisible and dim!

This is the paradox: we must beware the light, lest it lead us to darkness;
and we must welcome the darkness, that we might behold the light.

CHAPTER 3

The Ascetic Imagination

Fancy is involved in all things.

Xenophanes

Jesus, peace be upon him, struck the ground with his hand and took up some of it and spread it out, and behold, he had gold in one of his hands and clay in the other. Then he said to his companions, "Which of these is sweeter to your hearts?" They said, "The gold." He said, "They are both alike to me."

Islamic apophthegm

When my soul is in Eden with our first parents, I myself am there in a blessed manner. When I walk with Enoch, and see his translation, I am transported with him. The present age is too little to contain it. I can visit Noah in his ark, and swim upon the waters of the deluge. I can see Moses with his rod, and the children of Israel passing through the sea; I can enter into Aaron's Tabernacle, and admire the mysteries of the holy place. I can travel over the Land of Canaan, and see it overflowing with milk and honey; I can visit Solomon in his glory, and go into his temple, and view the sitting of his servants, and admire the magnificence of his kingdom.

Thomas Traherne

Seeing our imaginations have great power over our hearts, and can mightily affect us with their representations, it would be of great use to you if, at the beginning of your devotions, you were to imagine to yourself some such representations as might heat and warm your heart into a temper suitable to those prayers that you are then about to offer unto God.

William Law

Jesus uttered many strange sentences, but few stranger than those now found in Matthew 19:12: "There are eunuchs who have been so from birth, and there are eunuchs who have been made eunuchs by men, and there are eunuchs who have made themselves eunuchs for the sake of the kingdom of heaven. He who is able to receive this, let him receive it." I believe that these words (upon which I have never heard a sermon) were, originally, a brilliant riposte. Marriage was, for most first-century Jews, not an option but a divine obligation: "Be fruitful and multiply and fill the earth." Yet, notwithstanding *The Da Vinci Code* and other sensationalistic books written for the gullible, Jesus was certainly celibate. When one adds that Jesus' opponents slandered him ("friend of tax collectors and sinners," Matt. 11:19); that "eunuch" was sometimes a word of abuse hurled at unmarried men; and that Jesus, like Paul after him, regularly picked up opponents' rebukes, imaginatively remade them, and then handed them back, we may think this: Jesus, upon being jeered as a castrate, responded by inventing a new class of eunuchs, one established by and for heaven.

Whether or not my guess regarding the genesis of Matthew 19:12 is near the truth, Jesus, we may be sure, did not counsel self-mutilation. His disciples were not akin to the devotees of Cybele and Attis, who, in fits of religious ecstasy repugnant to us, ran through the streets holding aloft newly cut testicles. Jesus was a Jewish sage, and Jewish sages loved hyperbole, as in this saying from the Talmud: "If a man performs a single commandment, it shall be well with him and he shall have length of days and shall inherit the land. But if he neglects a single commandment, it shall be ill with him and he shall not have length of days and shall not inherit the land." Jesus everywhere spoke in exaggeration and metaphor, which means he spoke chiefly to the imagination. This is why a veil lies over the minds of those who proudly "take the Bible literally." Without the imagination, even those who begin with the Spirit will end with the flesh.

Unfortunately, the literalism of the fundamentalist is not new under the sun. Justin Martyr, writing to the Roman emperor in the middle of the second century, filed this curious story:

That you may understand that promiscuous intercourse is not one of our mysteries, one of our number a short time ago presented to

Felix the governor of Alexandria a petition, craving that permission might be given to a surgeon to make him a eunuch. For the surgeons there said that they were forbidden to do this without the permission of the governor. And when Felix absolutely refused to sign such a permission, the youth remained single, and was satisfied with his own approving conscience. . . .

That this incident was not isolated, and that some Christians successfully stopped their testosterone flow, appears from the records of the First Council of Nicea (A.D. 325), which passed legislation regarding ministers who had emasculated themselves: "If any one has been obliged to undergo a surgical operation from disease, or has been castrated by barbarians, let him continue in the clergy. But if any one in good health has so mutilated himself, it is right that, if he be enrolled among the clergy, he should cease from his ministrations" (canon 1). Happily, this judgment against castration, which rightly assumes a figurative interpretation of Matthew 19:12, is comfortably nested in all the major branches of Christendom.

But then there are always the twigs. Perhaps the most infamous episode in the sordid history of Christian castration took place relatively recently, in the eighteenth and nineteenth centuries. With the Russian Skoptsy sect, castration (dubbed "the baptism of fire") became a mass movement. For more than a century, thousands of men, supposing themselves to be doing something marvelous, rid themselves of their manhood, while the women, striving as ever for equality, imitated as best they could. Further details, preserved for morbid curiosity in the police records, I need not relate here.

Abelard (of Abelard and Heloise fame) affirmed, in the twelfth century A.D., that Origen of Alexandria, born a thousand years earlier, was "the greatest of Christian philosophers." This, from an accomplished theologian thoroughly acquainted with the entirety of Christian thinkers before him, including the mighty Augustine, is profound acclaim indeed. But the praise was earned.

Origen was the most learned philosopher of his day and attracted students from throughout the empire. His memory was prodigious. He carried around in his head most (and maybe all) of the books in our Bible, and some not in it. His literary output was equally prodigious, even fantastic. He was (if we exclude the rumors about the god Hermes, purported author of twenty thousand books) probably the most prolific writer in the ancient world, its Georges Simenon. His nickname was Adamantius, meaning "man of steel," with reference, it appears, to his phenomenal capacity for work. Jerome asked, "Who could read all his books?" Epiphanius said there were six thousand of them — clearly exaggeration, but still indicative.

Seven full-time stenographers, following Origen wherever he went, took turns insuring that no serious word failed to fall onto paper. Perhaps we should envisage him as a sort of Johnson or Coleridge, a master of the extemporaneous monologue. I also think of Richard Haney in Hitchcock's version of *The Thirty-Nine Steps;* for we have the record of one occasion on which Origen stood before a congregation, turned to ask the bishop upon which of the four texts just read the sermon should be spoken, and, upon receiving the answer, immediately delivered a rich and memorable homily.

Origen was the first textual critic and the first editor of a parallel Bible, the so-called Hexapla, a synopsis of different Hebrew and Greek versions of the Old Testament. And his most famous book, *On First Principles,* although not exactly a systematic theology, was the earliest effort to supply a comprehensive philosophical exposition of Christian doctrine. Origen's "researches" (his term) in this treatise and elsewhere, especially on the nature of God and the Trinity, were formative for all later theology. As testimony to his towering erudition and charismatic power, we have the words of Gregory Thaumaturgus, a student who declared that to quit Origen's presence was to leave Paradise and become a second Adam. This must be the highest compliment ever paid to a teacher.

Beyond the many good reasons that we understand, Origen was also esteemed, by pagans as well as by Christians, for his asceticism, a thing we do not understand. He managed, we are told, with very little sleep: night for him was an invitation to reading and prayer. When he did sleep, he reclined, like the samurai in another time and place, on the bare ground, with nothing under his head, except perhaps a rock. Origen also fasted severely, drank no wine, owned next to nothing, and went for years without shoes. As Eusebius, the first church historian, said, "He persevered in cold and nakedness." Like Francis of Assisi, but unlike the rich young ruler in the Gospels, he sold all that he had — including a large library inherited from his martyred father — and gave the proceeds to the poor.

Above all, however, Origen showed his contempt for earthly pleasure by having himself castrated. (This is about the only thing most people now know about him, which tells us less about Origen than about most people.) Here is how Eusebius recounted the tale:

> Understanding the expression, "There are eunuchs who have made themselves such for the sake of the kingdom of heaven," in too literal and puerile a sense, and at the same time thinking that he would fulfill the words of our Savior, while he also wished to preclude the unbelievers from all occasions of foul slander, it being necessary for him, young as he was, to converse on divine truth not only with men but with females also, he was led on to fulfill the words of our Savior by his deeds. . . .

This story does not recommend its hero. Disbelief first and disgust second are our reaction. We suppose that, if Origen did indeed so act (some have doubted the story), he must have been a fanatic, or worse.

This, however, will not do. Origen did not have a sick brain. Quite the contrary: he was, as his contemporaries recognized, and as those who still read him know full well, an authentic genius, a man of monumental achievement and industry. Although the later (and unfortunate) condemnation of some of his teachings by fifth- and sixth-century church councils has clouded his reputation, and although the burning of most of his books by anti-Origenist monks has left us with all too little, the truth is that he was one of the world's great thinkers. I hesitate to assign the actions of such a one to religious neurosis, or to conjecture, on the basis not of evidence but of modern psychology, that the man must have had introjected hostile feelings toward his world, come to resent his ego, and finally punished himself. Such conjecture is just too easy. Does not Origen teach us more about human nature than that it is sometimes its own enemy?

Origen was one of many. That is, numerous early Christians shared his ascetic habits. Many refused to marry or, although married, gave up conjugal rights. Many ate as little as possible, and nothing at all for certain periods. Many had no possessions. When the monastic movement bloomed in Egypt at the beginning of the fourth century, with Anthony's trek into the Egyptian desert, Christianity's roots were already ascetic. Men and women questing for God took for granted a life of the strictest self-denial. This was especially true in Syria, where ascetic practices seem to have been the most extreme. Syria in any case was home to Simeon Stylites (ca. 390-459), the first of the pillar-sitters.

Simeon, according to his friend, Theodoret of Cyrrhus, was "the great wonder of the world." Theodoret prefaced his little biography with this:

> I myself, though having all men, so to speak, as witnesses of his contests that beggar description, am afraid that the narrative may seem to posterity to be a myth totally devoid of truth. For the facts surpass human nature, and men are wont to use nature to measure what is said: if anything is said that lies beyond the limits of nature, the account is judged to be false by those uninitiated into divine things.

Simeon was born in the little village of Sisa and, like King David, grew up shepherding his parents' flock. But one Sunday in church he heard the Gospel that blesses those who "mourn and weep" (Luke 6:25), and he thereafter chose the solitary life. He joined a group of eighty ascetics and lived among them ten years. During that time he surpassed them all in severity. They, for example, fasted only every other day, he for a week at a time. Eventually the elders asked Simeon to leave. His self-tortures, which included tying a coarse cord around his waist so tightly that it bled, were, it seems, thought excessive, inappropriate inspiration for the young.

Simeon, after being expelled, retreated to the solitude of a tiny cottage. One day it entered his head to undertake a great fast, in imitation of Moses and Elijah and Jesus. He urged a friendly priest to seal with clay the door to his cell and not to return for forty days and forty nights. The priest, unwilling to sponsor suicide, declared himself an assistant only if he could leave ten rolls and a jar of water. This was allowed, and Simeon was sealed in.

When the allotted time had passed, the clay was broken and the door opened. The rolls were still there. So too the jug of water, yet full. Simeon himself was prostrate, unable to speak or move. But after the priest rinsed his mouth and gave him communion, he stirred, opened his eyes, and slowly climbed his way back to the land of the living.

After this achievement Simeon subsequently made every Lenten fast a complete fast. Theodoret informs us that, the first few times he tried this, he stood for several days, then sat down, and ended on his back. But after years of practice, Simeon "reduced much of the pain" and in fact could stand unsupported the whole time. No wonder Theodoret opened his narrative by prophesying doubters. (Let me add, however, that the modern medical literature does document fasts of thirty, forty, and even fifty days, although to my knowledge none of these excluded water. There are also the twentieth-century Catholic inedics, such as the German stigmatist Therese Neumann and the French invalid Marthe Robin, whose ability to live on nothing except communion is, if I can believe what I read, avouched by skeptical physicians. So maybe it is not impossible that Simeon duplicated the feat of the male emperor penguin, which during its six weeks of brooding stands and takes no food.)

Simeon, after living in his cottage for three years, moved to a nearby hilltop. There he passed the remainder of his days. Initially he chained himself to a rock, like a dog on a leash. But as his fame grew, as people came to him for advice, prayer, and healing, as the crowds swelled and the roads to his plateau became like rivers with pilgrims from throughout the Roman Empire and beyond, the saint invented the notion of standing on a pillar, upon which was set a square platform (six feet by six feet), open to the elements. The column was at first only a few feet high. By his death, however, it reached over sixty feet. For, to quote Theodoret, Simeon "yearned to fly up to heaven and to be separated from this life on earth."

Raised on his pillar, Simeon became a spectacle. He ate just once a week. He forsook sleep. He stood night and day, moving only to bend his waist in worship. (He had others bind his feet to a pillar so he could never recline.) We understand why a man once asked Simeon, "Are you a man or a bodiless being . . . ? I hear everyone repeating that you neither eat nor lie down, both of which are proper to men — for no one with a human nature could live without sleep and food."

Let me here end the story-telling and turn to the inevitable question: Why? Why did Origen castrate himself? Why did Simeon stand on a pillar, unprotected from the weather? And why did countless others do similar alarming things and lead lives of apparent misery? Why did Macarius of Alexandria attempt to stay awake for twenty days? Why did a certain Macedonius eat nothing but ground barley soaked in water? Why did Limnaeus the Syrian pass his entire adult life inside a roofless circle of stones? Why did Thalelaeus spend a decade as a living "V," bent double between two planks of wood?

Despite my earlier remarks on Origen, I am tempted to think that some of these people *were,* as was Henry Suso, the medieval German mystic, beset by mental illness. (Maybe a few even suffered from what is now called DSH — Deliberate Self-Harm Syndome.) Yet, even supposing so, that explains neither why their pathology took the form it did, nor why such people were revered as near gods — revered not only by the Christian laity but also by many well-educated pagans (the famous physician Galen, for instance). Christian apologists such as Justin Martyr and Eusebius actually bragged to outsiders about Christian austerity and abstinence.

There is in addition the further circumstance that asceticism is not unique to early Christianity — we have all heard of the medieval flagellants — or even to Christianity. Legend has it that the Buddha, before enlightenment, sat on thorns and subsisted on a single grain of rice a day (which is why some Thai statues allow such easy counting of Gautama's ribs). Hinduism's Laws of Manu prescribe that the fourth and final stage of a man's life should be characterized by poverty, worldly indifference, and great austerity; and the ascetic ethic of Jainism, which teaches that one should, upon feeling the end to be near, extinguish all karma through a fast unto death, is notorious. Obviously there is more to be said.

In all times and places men and women have sought to do out-of-the-ordinary things, and, as William James has pointed out, "it is usual to human nature to court the arduous." The first half of the twentieth century had wing-walkers, while the second half had motorcycle daredevils. The explanation is twofold. First, exhilaration accompanies extraordinary behavior, especially behavior that tempts death; and who does not desire exhilaration? Second, such behavior breeds notoriety. Buster Keaton, Sir Edmund Hillary, and Karl Wallenda are well-known names.

It was no different in the ancient world. We think of Simeon and his kin as recluses, which they were not. The famous Saint Anthony, after moving to the Egyptian desert, was not forever alone. Disciples followed after him. Barren women sought him out for healing. And the curious went to listen to his strange screams as he battled with devils. Anthony was never truly alone — which explains why we have his story.

So too Simeon. Despite his apparent attempts to seek God in private, he ended his life as a rural patron, religious oracle, and public sensation. His feats, including never-ending prayer, were a sort of holy entertainment; and his racked but unbowed body was a vicarious transformation that opened imaginations to new possibilities. Beyond this, because he literally stood outside the boundaries of ordinary society, and because he had no familial or political or economic ties, Simeon was what every community needs: the perfectly impartial judge. Each day a flood of humanity rose about his pillar, and he became a one-man court of law. Emperor, bishop, and peasant alike sought and followed the counsel of Simeon Stylites. As a recent commentator has put it, "This holy man ran an extensive social-service network from the top of his pillar." Looking down from the heights, the naked, starving man in bonds, who wore his soul on the outside, ruled the world as the living symbol of the crucified Christ.

The one who threw all power and influence upon the waters saw them come back to him, and multiplied a thousandfold. One would like to know if Simeon anticipated as much, whether he knew of what Edward Gibbon called "the secret road which led to the possession of wealth and honours." It is plain at least that he did not really wish to be alone, for standing upon a pillar does not constitute hiding. One has to ask: Were his deeds, and those of his fellow athletes, partially motivated by the knowledge that one might find strength by losing it? There are many ways to fame; and if one could not rise in the church through excellence in studies or by elevation to ecclesiastical office, asceticism was yet another route to the goal of repute and influence.

There must, I think, be some truth in this cynical reading of the evidence. The fancy for fame infects us all, and, in Simeon's time and place, to sow extreme asceticism was to reap renown. Yet this fact fills the bucket of understanding only a little. For while the longing for renown is universal, extreme asceticism is not. Leaving aside David Blaine, whose strange activities are designed as public stunts, pillar-sitters have ceased to be. (The last one I know of was seen in nineteenth-century Russian Georgia.) The fate of fasting in the Roman Catholic Church tells the same story: bodily austerity is no longer popular. So we must wonder what made the ancient world so very different from ours. What made it quench its thirst for novelty in extreme asceticism rather than in something else? And why is it that we, heirs of the Reformation and the Enlightenment, have so little empathy for the old ascetics and their harsh habits? Why has the once mighty and magnificent oak of asceticism become a rotting stump?

Religious experience, which our ancestors trusted more than we do, is one component of the answer. When one refuses to sleep, or suffers extreme pain, or eliminates sensory stimuli, visions may ensue. Visions may also follow fasting (or, more precisely, if I recall correctly, vitamin B-6 deprivation). And, if one knows this, visions may be artificially induced. When Simeon entered his great fast, he deprived his senses. No food. No drink. No sound. No light. I am nearly certain that, in such a state, the monk saw visions and dreamed dreams. The extant biographies do not, I concede, confirm this (although they do report that, on other occasions, Simeon prayed away serpents and dragons). But abundant sources document that, for ascetics in general, the vision was a religious staple. Anthony, it is reported to our disbelief, passed many a night talking to the devil, and as Athanasius tells us,

> when once he had a conversation with someone who visited him about the soul's passage, and its location after this life, the next night someone called to him from above, saying, "Anthony, get up — go out and look!" Going out . . . he saw someone huge, and ugly and fearsome, standing and reaching the clouds — and certain beings ascending as if they had wings. And the high figure extended his hands, and some were being held back by him, but others, flying upwards and finally passing him by, ascended without anxiety. That great one gnashed his teeth over those latter, but over those who fell back he rejoiced.

Those who value visions must also value the means of obtaining them. It follows that early Christians valued asceticism. Like the Siberian shaman who eats psychoactive mushrooms, and like the Amerindian medicine man who induces mystical visions with peyote, the early Christian ascetics obviously prized experience of another world — prized it so much that they happily bought it at the price of severe physical deprivation and pain. Days without food, weeks without sleep, years without sitting: do any of our contemporary athletes have the physical courage or mental stamina displayed by Simeon Stylites and his imitators (of which there were many)? However that may be, I am reminded of what a woman who underwent a so-called near-death experience told me: Although she has no plans for suicide, her experience was so unspeakably wonderful that death has lost its sting, and she would like a repeat. Obviously, certain extraordinary mental events can be craved.

Let me add that I question the modern habit of dismissing as "subjective" all artificially induced experiences. "Yes, if you eat too little, you see visions, and if you drink too much, you see snakes." So Bertrand Russell. But just because our language has the word "hallucination," which we throw at a very large class of experiences — the surgical patient's out-of-body experience, Aristotle's vision of his *Doppelgänger*, my wife's hypnagogic faces, Tesla's visual memories that appeared in front of his eyes, the black shadow of the Old Hag phenomenon written up by David Hufford, the illusions summoned by hypnotists — understanding is not thereby assured. We have in truth no real comprehension of the most basic fact of all, consciousness. It remains, in Karl Popper's words, "the greatest of miracles." Despite the travail of so many philosophers and scientists, we have not fulfilled the Delphic command to know ourselves. Furthermore, I suspect (in part because of personal experience) that C. D. Broad and Aldous Huxley were right to urge that the brain is a reducing valve. Like the eye, which perceives only a portion of the electromagnetic spectrum, the brain may restrict experience; and when it is altered (as by drugs or malnourishment), the mind may sometimes find itself catching confused glimpses of other planes of existence: as Huxley put it, the "lowering of what may be called the biological efficiency of the brain seems to permit the entry into consciousness of certain classes of mental events, which are normally excluded, because they possess no survival value." We now know, from study of schizophrenics, that endorphins at any rate can filter out environmental messages on their way to consciousness.

The religious experiences of early Christians confirmed their dualistic philosophy: they believed in a world beyond this one. Their habit, moreover, was to believe that other world a better place (although, to judge by the extant records, they tended to see more demons than angels). Under the impact of a pessimism abroad in late antiquity and a forceful Platonism — which together taught that "the corporeal must be burdensome and heavy, earthly and visible; it is by this that . . . a soul is weighed down and dragged back to the visible world" (Plato) — matter and sin became intertwined. Although the church confessed God the Father to be the Maker of heaven and earth, confessed God the Son to have been made man, and confessed belief in the resurrection of the body, human flesh was not esteemed. Origen may have affirmed that "in itself bodily nature is not involved in evil," but he lived like a Stoic, combatting the flesh. Despite the wise restraints put on hyperasceticism by Ambrose, Augustine, Basil the Great, and Benedict, Plato's Pythagorean legacy, that "the body leads us astray," was as ingrained then as the goodness of "self-esteem" is now. Ignatius could write, "Nothing visible is good." Anthony, according to Athanasius, felt disgraced before he slept or attended to other bodily necessities; and "he would blush if seen eating by others." Like the Neoplatonic pagan Plotinus, Anthony was obviously "ashamed of being in the body."

One searches early Christian literature almost in vain for the joy of Psalm 104: "Thou makest springs gush forth in the valleys; they flow between the hills, they give drink to every beast of the field; the wild asses quench their thirst" (vv. 10-11). With the exception of Theophylact Simocatta and a passage near the end of Augustine's *City of God* (22.24), and perhaps a few others in the writings of Gregory of Nyssa, I do not know of old Christian texts that revel in Nature. Who, like St. Francis, sang to sun and moon? The spirit of Plato's *Phaedo* haunted the Christians: the pleasures of the soul were at war with the pleasures of the body. In such a context, asceticism was natural, and Christianity became a spiritual Sparta. Tertullian, at the end of the second century, bragged that, because they enjoy what God has made, Christians do not number among themselves Brahmans or Indian gymnosophists. His boast may or may not have been justified when made, but a hundred and fifty years later it certainly would have sounded ridiculous.

If the old dualistic worldview, which was as much moral as ontological, distances most of us from the early Christians, there is an even more profound reason why asceticism is disagreeable to us but was appealing to them. We oppose pneumonia with antibiotics, overcome drought with dams and irrigation, fight infertility with artificial insemination. We have, with our technology, come close to fulfilling Adam's divine mission: "Fill the earth and subdue it." Not so our ancestors. When confronted by plague, they prayed. When the rains ceased, they prayed. When a woman was barren, they prayed. In other words, they were helpless before Nature's whims. We, with our eyeglasses and birth-control devices, take for granted a freedom utterly foreign to those before us. (This is one reason we pray less than they did.)

Early Christian recommendations of virginity, which regularly refer to the shame of infertility, the pain of birth, and the high rate of infant mortality, help us appreciate the servitude of past generations. When Jerome wrote of "the womb growing larger for nine months, the sickness, the delivery, the blood, the swaddling clothes," he used the expression "the humiliations of Nature." Gregory of Nyssa remarked that when a woman's labor comes, "the occasion is not regarded as the bringing of a child into the world but as the approach of death; in bearing it is expected that she will die." And when she does, there are "bitter outbursts against human destiny, arraigning of the whole course of Nature, complaints and accusations even against the divine government."

For those in olden times, when plagues were so common and remedies so few, the body, especially that of woman, was slave to ills innumerable. But human beings have always hungered for freedom. That is why they have built shelters, pronounced magic spells, and flown in their dreams.

Early Christians were no different. Indeed, the pangs within them were sharpened by their theology, which held that Christ had inaugurated a new age, that the kingdom of God had come. According to 2 Timothy, Hymenaeus and Philetus pushed "realized eschatology" to the peculiar conclusion "that the resurrection is past already" (2:18).

While we know nothing further about them or their beliefs, the New Testament itself taught Christians that they had somehow been crucified to the world and raised with Christ. Did it not follow that believers could be "like the angels in heaven" and so live above both Nature and the decaying social order?

Nietzsche was wrong to allege that Christian asceticism was fostered by an excessive humility promoted by the Gospels. Rather, just like its antithesis, Gnostic and Carpocratian libertinism, the ascetic movement was a daring and perhaps inevitable experiment designed to show the triumph of eschatology over history, redemption over Nature, grace over necessity. Gregory wanted "to change flesh to spirit." Origen exhorted, "Resolve to know that in you there is capacity to be transformed." Evagrius wrote of Simeon, "This man, endeavoring to realize in the flesh the existence of heavenly hosts, lifts himself above the concerns of each, and, overpowering the downward tendency of human nature, is intent upon things above: placed between heaven and earth, he holds communion with God, and unites with the angels in praising him."

Asceticism was, as Peter Brown has so expertly taught us, the knife by which monks and nuns cut their bonds to the natural course of things. Fasting created independence from the marketplace and immunity to famine. The renunciation of possessions placed one outside the social order and became an anchor against all economic ebb and flow. And the refusal to beget children arrested the reproductive cycle and forestalled many potential calamities. Detachment meant freedom — the freedom to be in the world, but not of it. Hermes Trismegistus declared, "If a man holds aloof from the desires of this world, the misfortunes of this world hold aloof from him." Orwell, although unsympathetic, knew the truth: "The main motive for 'nonattachment' is a desire to escape from the pain of living."

Our ever-increasing independence from the forces and cycles of Nature — an independence which renders superfluous the attempt to gain freedom through extreme asceticism — is, in the end, only the conclusion of the ascetic project. For we are using machines to finish what Origen and the others began. Our quest for safety and comfort makes us heirs to their task, and like them we apply our ingenuity to cast off the burdens of the natural world.

If our continuity of purpose engenders empathy, so too should the knowledge that our spiritual forebears mined their physical freedom for the treasure of a mental freedom. If we can raise ourselves up to see past our modern prejudices, past our incessant psychologizing and doubts about supernatural beings, we shall behold the obvious: the old Christian ascetics were trophys of the imagination. (I like the definition of George William Russell: "Imagination is not a vision of something which already exists" but an internal speech and sight by which "what exists in latency or essence is out-realised and is given a form in thought," so that we "can contemplate with full consciousness that which hitherto had been unrevealed, or only intuitionally surmised.") Imagination is the true continuity between the ascetics and Jesus, the Jewish sage who, although he saw neither a camel being swallowed nor one going through the eye of a needle, spoke about them both.

Origen forged a beautiful and compelling philosophical synthesis by linking together ideas theretofore unlinked. Anthony, although not the first anchorite, inaugurated a revolution by transferring monastic life from the edges of communities to the isolated desert. As for Simeon, no one has yet produced evidence that there were pillar-sitters before him. Despite the inevitable scholarly search for parallels, he, as Theodoret claimed, evidently invented the idea: "Never has such a thing happened anywhere, that a man should go up and live on a pillar."

If the imagination is not only, as Mary Warnock (following Hume and Kant) has urged, an ingredient in all perception and cognition, but also, as more popularly conceived, the engine of all creativity, then Origen and Athanasius and Simeon had imagination in abundance. We are likely to miss this because the ascetic tradition, for obvious reason, said otherwise. Not only did it want to assign its happy revelations to God and the angels rather than fantasy, but celibate monks who consumed gruel were obviously tormented by visions of naked dancing girls and elaborate banquets. Maximus the Confessor, it is unsurprising to learn, claimed that Adam, before his fall, altogether lacked an imagination; and Nicodemus of the Holy Mountain, one of the editors of the modern *Philokalia*, said

the same of Christ: being omniscient, the Savior had no need of imagination and therefore had none. (This must be unwitting heresy, for it makes
Jesus less than "fully human.") Pseudo-Dionysius observed that, if anyone
has "reckless imagination," it must be the devil. Obviously the scriptural
words about "vain imaginings" rang true for many.

But they do not sound the same to us. We believe, as John of the
Cross expressed it, that we come to the imagination "as though to a sea-
port or market to buy and sell provisions. . . . God and the devil come
here with the jewels of images and supernatural forms to offer." In other
words, the imagination is the gamut of creative possibilities, good and
bad. This is why Einstein could famously say, "Imagination is better than
knowledge."

Jesus, so long ago, must already have thought or intuited the same
thing. Why else did he give us not rules but parables and images? (There
is only one rule in the Sermon on the Mount, that on divorce.) And why
else did he accost the well-versed Pharisees with, "Have you not read?"
Of course they had read, and that a thousand times. Jesus was indicting
not their ignorance but their imaginations: hearing, they did not hear.
Their minds were inert.

I was once told, on good authority, that, somewhere in the *Philokalia*
of Nicodemus, Eve's sin is assigned to her lack of imagination: she saw
only an apple, not what it meant. I have been unable to verify this. But I
do know that at least William Blake and Charles Williams diagnosed sin
as that lack; and I think we should take up their teaching. For theological
thinking and religious behavior both depend upon our magical ability to
transcend the given.

If we leave aside the strange vision in Exodus 33 (Moses saw the back
of God) and ignore Jesus as in a category to himself, then, as John's Gospel says, no one has seen God at any time. And yet Christians incessantly
talk to and about God. How is this possible? Christians also speak much
about heaven and hell, but how many have been to those places, except in
their analogy-constructing imaginations? These last may feed upon sense
perception; but they are not what they eat. When the psalmist sang that
the Lord makes the clouds his chariot and rides upon the wings of the
winds, he was using his imagination.

And what of prayer? Or worship? Western and Eastern Christians have traditionally interpreted their services, as did the sect of the Dead Sea Scrolls, as participation in the heavenly liturgy: they are raised to heaven, and heaven comes down to them. As it says in the *Liturgy of Chrysostom*, "O Master, Lord our God, who hast appointed in heaven orders and hosts of angels and archangels for the service of thy glory: cause that with our entrance there may be an entrance of holy angels serving with us and glorifying thy goodness." But how is this reality to be perceived, if not with the same faculty that allowed Bosch to paint hell and Dante to write of heaven?

Many are of course loath to admit the obvious, for fear that Feuerbach and Freud will win out: maybe all of religion is a placebo, or the pathetic fallacy writ large. Montaigne declared, "It is probable that the belief in miracles, visions, enchantments, and such extraordinary occurrences springs in the main from the power of the imagination acting principally on the minds of the common people, who are the more easily impressed." But the truth remains what it is. As Blake said, "Imagination is spiritual sensation." Faith is the assurance of things hoped for, the conviction of things not seen, and its eye is the religious imagination.

The old ascetics taught themselves to keep that eye focused. They passed most of their time contemplating things they could neither remember nor perceive with their five senses. That left them imagination — which explains why they uttered parables, saw visions, posed riddles, and kept silence. They were like cosmologists and subatomic physicists, who explore regions too large or too small to be perceived, and like the writers of science fiction, who narrate the unborn future. Exploration of any world beyond that of physical eyes and ears requires a creative internal perception.

Yeats commented that William Blake, who was so often by internal vision rapt, "spoke confusedly and obscurely . . . because he spoke of things for whose speaking he could find no models in the world he knew." It is the same with us and the verities of our faith, as Paul explained when he spoke of seeing through a glass darkly. Not only is all meaning invisible, but neither things transcendent nor things future can be recalled, and reason cannot entrap them. "All our knowledge of God is symbolic," Kant said, and theology is the study of inadequate metaphors. Is God a rock? A father? A shepherd? Well, not really, but sort of. We can never pass beyond Socrates' "this or something like it." The higher our language climbs, the more slippery the rungs. Confusion and obscurity are our lot, apophatic theology — the theology of negation — our truth. John Damascene observed, "It is impossible to say what God is in Himself, and it is more exact to speak of Him by excluding everything"; and Aquinas completed the point by saying that "what He is not is clearer to us than what He is." And yet: to see through a glass darkly is still to see — for which we may thank the imagination, which is that glass.

In addition to living in two worlds at once, and thereby prodding what Arthur Koestler called bisociative thinking, the ascetics (although this is hardly what they took themselves to be doing) cultivated imagination by forsaking buildings and streets. Anthony went into the desert; and one source speaks of "the wildness of the spot" where Simeon sat on his pillar. Despite the many important differences, something is here shared with the Romantic poets (a natural comparison, as so much of Christianity is poetry). The Romantics exalted, almost deified, the imagination, celebrated the natural world, and taught that the latter fashions the former, that the landscape sculpt the inscape.

The first condition for seeing "Proteus rising from the sea," or for hearing "old Triton blow his wreathéd horn," is "standing on this pleasant lea." Blake may have lived mostly in London, but only of necessity, and he hated it. Wordsworth ("nine-tenths of my verses have been murmured out in the open air") dwelt in the Lake District. So too, for a considerable time, Coleridge — who, in "Frost at Midnight," promised his infant son that he would not live "in the great city, pent 'mid cloisters dim" but rather

> wander like a breeze
> By lakes and sandy shores, beneath the crags
> Of ancient mountain, and beneath the clouds.

Wordsworth taught that the imagination, given to us "to incite and to support the eternal," is at its height when manipulating images of the natural world; and one of his poems bears this cumbersome title: "Influence of Natural Objects in Calling Forth and Strengthening the Imagination in Boyhood and Early Youth." Blake wrote that "to the eyes of the man of Imagination, Nature is Imagination itself." I am unsure what that means, but I doubt not that uncivilized environments nourished the creative powers of the cenobites and anchorites (even though their attitude toward nature was far less romantic than ours). Abba Hyperechius said, "As the lion is terrible to wild asses, so is the experienced monk to desires."

C. H. Dodd notes that the parables of Jesus presuppose that "there is no mere analogy, but an inward affinity, between the natural order and the spiritual order." If this is so, then Nature is latent with divinely implanted meaning and must point beyond itself to an invisible realm. Experience teaches many of us that it does. And the statistics in Alister Hardy's *The Spiritual Nature of Man* offer verification. After "prayer and meditation" and (interestingly enough) "depression, despair," the most common trigger of "feelings of a religious kind" is "natural beauty." As one whose foundational religious experience took place not in a church but under the stars with no one around, I doubt the proposition — which became dogma in the nineteenth century, and is today taken for granted — that Nature is passive.

> We receive but what we give,
> And in our life alone does Nature live.

Was Coleridge wholly right about this?

One of my undergraduate philosophy professors, a confident atheist, once confided that years before, on a late afternoon, in a sun-drenched glade, he was overwhelmed by beauty and, for a few minutes, was compelled, against his habit, to believe in a divine artist. While he soon wielded rationalism to amputate the newfound conviction, the experience itself — in which the percipient felt wholly passive — was undeniable and is common enough.

One remembers the story of Edgar Mitchell on Apollo 14. The sight of the earth from afar, a blue-and-white jewel against black velvet space, made "palpable" the presence of divinity and altered the course of his life: "I knew that life in the universe was not just an accident based on random processes. This knowledge came to me directly — noetically. It was not a matter of discursive reasoning or logical abstraction. It was an experiential cognition." Nature brings a lore that tells of more than the aesthetic, a lore that, like a spark in a powder keg, will (if the powder is not too wet) ignite the religious imagination. Paul was not naïve in asserting that God has been "clearly perceived in the things that have been made" (Rom. 1:20).

If certain contemplative practices and a nearness to Nature enlarged the ascetic imagination, surely the savage solitude of the desert did, too; for, as Aquinas pointed out, "when a soul is abstracted from bodily realities it is more adapted to coming under the sway of spiritual substances; it is also more sensitive to those subtle impressions which natural causes leave upon the human imagination." Those who fled the cities praised silence as much as they praised God. Deafness was a virtue, a monastic community a collection of shattered gongs. One fourth-century observer, Rufinus, noted that cenobites lived far apart so as not to hear each other; and he bore witness to "a huge silence and a great quiet." Abba Arsenius, when in "silent prayer," even disliked the sound of reeds in the wind. I would wager that his life was proof of what Gregory Thaumaturgus said, that "silence is indeed the friend and helpmeet of thought and invention." Maimonides expressed himself similarly: "The principal and highest function" of the imagination — which he admittedly defined in the restricted sense as all inner representations — "is performed when the senses are at rest and pause in their action." The unfathomed imagination has its own eyes and ears, and they are most alert when the physical eyes and ears are put to bed. As Wordsworth had it: when "the light of sense" goes out, or the body is "laid asleep," then we "become a living soul."

Although Origen and Anthony and Simeon remain strangers to our time, of and from them we may still learn much. Not only can we glimpse some of their motives, but their stories, which sometimes make for such alarming reading, write a still-valid prescription for fortifying the imagination. It has three parts: (1) extended reflection upon transcendent realities, (2) prolonged experience of the natural world, and (3) stillness without and within. Asceticism may seem opposed to justification by faith (so Luther and Calvin — but not, notably, Augustine); and certainly self-mortification, in a culture predicated upon the fulfillment of wants defined as needs, is no longer good missionary strategy. (In the harsh world of late antiquity, on the contrary, healthy, well-fed monks would have been ignored by a populace accustomed to famine, plague, war, and poverty.) But Max Scheler was right: despite its undeniable defects, asceticism was "positive, not negative" because it "fundamentally aspired to liberate the highest powers of personality from obstruction by the automatism of the lower drives." And that aspiration should remain ours.

But if the desert Christians wisely remade their environments so as to free their internal senses, we seem foolishly to be doing just the opposite. First, enthralled by the ever-expanding possibilities of technology, many of us are materialists in theory, most of us materialists in fact: this world is our home, and here our minds rest.

Second, we are — and this takes us back to the introductory chapter — more and more removed from Nature because we spend more and more time within our artificial environments. In day-to-day urban life, Nature is more a ghost than a bodily presence. We now live largely "inside" (the setting for almost all of the horror stories produced in the nineteenth century, when people still instinctively knew the dangers of deserting Nature).

Third, if, in classical Aristotelian physics, rest is the natural state, in the human physics of modernity, all tends away from stillness and quiet, and we are, while awake, soaked with a torrent of audio and visual stimuli. We no longer hear the silence of angels.

These three circumstances, together a despotic triumvirate, now suppress us. How to demonstrate the resultant lethargy of imagination I do not know. But lethargy there must be. As Chesterton, speaking of both physical and intellectual stamina, already observed in 1908, "The chief mark of our epoch is a profound laziness and fatigue."

American Protestantism is surely symptomatic. It is easy to accept the liberal critique of fundamentalism: that it gives up the present for the past. But it is equally easy to accept the fundamentalist critique of liberalism: that it gives up the past for the present. In truth, our two defining "isms," so bereft of creative tension, suffer from the identical malady: constricted thinking. Although the two are enamored of different Delilahs, both have been shorn of their imaginations and so of their strength. The same holds for the rest of us, who can locate ourselves somewhere on a line between the two extremes. We are like the living points in A. E. Abbott's *Flatland:* all we do is move up and down the one-dimensional line. Is it too much to suggest that the Protestant imagination lies in the grave, awaiting resurrection?

Jesus Christ was, according to Blake, the perfect man ("the human form divine") because in him the imaginative principle had its most perfect expression. The theologoumenon appeals: Jesus of Nazareth obviously had imagination in abundance, and to that faculty he addressed himself. This does not, to be sure, imply that imagination is sufficient unto itself. Its images and abstractions should (although Blake would not have agreed) be framed by the four legs of Methodism — Scripture, tradition, reason, and experience. And yet the frame exists for the sake of the picture. It follows that there is an imperative to imitate Origen and Anthony and Simeon, to crave their creative capacities. If science advances through inspired exercise of the imagination — through Archimedes' association of a hot bath with the measurement of solids, through Galileo's ability to envisage motion without friction, through Newton's intuition to link the orbit of the moon with the fall of an apple — then how much more our religion, which must link the finite to the infinite?

Indeed, we are here haunted by the *imitatio Dei.* Coleridge, in a famous formulation indebted to Schelling, urged that the "primary imagination" is "the living Power and prime Agent of all human Perception . . . a repetition in the finite mind of the elemental act of creation in the infinite I AM." But that "living Power and prime Agent" can be (as Coleridge mournfully observed in "Dejection: An Ode") more or less vigorous; and that largely depends upon our care. God has planted a garden of imagination in the Eden of our hearts, and it is ours to till and to keep.

WORD

CHAPTER 4

The Fate of the Book

Should anyone of our nation be questioned about the laws, he would repeat them all more readily than his own name. The result, then, of our thorough grounding in the laws from the first dawn of intelligence is that we have them, as it were, engraven on our souls.

Josephus

From childhood you have been acquainted with the sacred writings.

2 Timothy 3:15

The proper study of mankind is books.

Aldous Huxley

What will happen to the book? The purveyors of doom proclaim, Yet forty years and books shall be destroyed. Night comes, when no one will read. Papyrus and its descendants are done for. Information is moving from books to chips. People are reading less and less. More and more they are watching screens — TV screens, movie screens, computer screens. The ax has been laid to the root of book learning; our old pages are chaff that the technological wind drives away.

But there is the other side, too. Maybe the textual apocalypse is not at hand. Barnes and Noble seems to be doing quite well lately. So too Amazon.com. The hyperbolists and doomsayers we always have with us. The book, in the age of the personal computer, prospers. Lots and lots of people are buying lots and lots of books, and will they not always do so? The tide is full; the sea of books has not withdrawn. This is not the horse and buggy we are talking about. Books are rather like clothing: fashions may change, but we are never going to go naked.

Truth is, the future is fog, and nobody knows if books have had it. The facts will appear only when the things to come have come and gone. In the meantime, only the one who can count the sands of the sea knows very much. I certainly know nothing of the future, not even whether there will be one. It is possible that, in a thousand years, only ancient historians will remember paper books. For all I know, education will then be by direct injection into the cerebral cortex. It is equally possible that in a thousand years large numbers will still be pondering printed editions of *Macbeth*. Who knows?

So let us prudently eschew speculation about the future and consider instead the present, where things are clearer because closer to hand. People may indeed still be reading books, but who is reading Scripture? Although of the making and selling of many Bibles there is no end, appearances can be deceiving. One can buy a book, turn a few pages, and then turn on the TV. It must happen all the time. A publisher recently asked me to review a lengthy manuscript. I said that the potential book, a triumph of tedium, should be banished to perdition. I confessed that I could never read more than ten pages without seeking relief in the TV. The miserable thing was published anyway. I guess it will sell: it has a pretty cover. Yet how many copies will be well-worn? Not many, I would wager.

One also suspects that much of the contemporary biblical trade is in gift Bibles — confirmation gifts, graduation gifts, and so forth — and one can ask how many such share the fate of high-school yearbooks: forever kept but scarcely touched. The encouraging sales do not prove that we are laying up Scripture in our hearts. Not long ago a pollster sought to gauge the biblical literacy of the North American public. One of his multiple-choice questions concerned the identity of Joan of Arc (this was before her TV appearance a few years back). Ten percent thought that Joan of Arc was Noah's wife.

We should perhaps not much trust polls, this one included. I am surprised it was only 10 percent. But whatever the numbers, do not Christian ministers constantly complain that their congregations do not delight in the law of the Lord, that they do not meditate on that law day and night? And of course, if one goes outside the church, the post-Christian amnesia is unspeakable. Once, in a college class in the middle of the Bible Belt, I passingly referred to Adam and Eve, after which a student asked me to quit dropping names without explaining them. Another student in the same class asked me about Paul, saying that he did not know much about him, just that he was one of those guys in the Old Testament. My two stellar students represent an ever-growing multitude. The same pollster who asked about Joan of Arc discovered that 40 percent of his respondents thought most of the Hebrew Bible was written *after* the Crucifixion.

The situation appears to be desperate. It is easy to throw up one's hands, and I would not counsel anyone to do otherwise. I threw up my hands many years ago. It is the only reasonable response to this second coming of pre-Reformation illiteracy.

I could justify my surrender to despair with sundry observations about books in general. I could, for example, observe that the Bible is a book, and then argue that its fate is bound up with the fate of all other books; and further that the Jeremiahs who contend that it is time to close the book on books are after all correct, and that when all books go away, ours will go away too. We could indeed get dramatic here. Maybe the old sociologists who were so sure about the obsolescence of religion were correct, albeit for the wrong reason. Maybe, when the churches shuffle off their holy book and become nothing more than sites on the Internet, the gates of Hades will have prevailed.

I could also muse about the fallen glory of books, how their mass production has, according to the principle of inflation, made them less valuable. I once worked in a bookstore, and a woman came in who wished to buy some books. I said, "What are you looking for?" She said, "Oh, I don't know, maybe some hardbacks — nothing too expensive." I patiently responded, "Could you be more specific?" She answered, "Well, I'm decorating, you know, and I need some books for my shelves; maybe fifty."

I might further, in promoting cynicism, regale you with horror stories about growing illiteracy — I once had a student ask me what a novelist is — or review the studies showing what no one but a fool could ever have doubted: that staring at a black-and-white page of unadorned print is pretty boring to those habituated to the colorful graven images of sitcoms, *Star Wars,* and GameBoy.

But all this has been discussed elsewhere. In this chapter it is my purpose to consider the fate not of all books but of one book, the church's book, the Bible. I could make any number of points. There are a hundred reasons for the demise of the Scriptures. And, parenthetically, many of them I do not mourn. We have needed to change some of our opinions about what the Bible is and what it does. In the following pages, however, I venture rather to assay some of the debilitating changes. In good homiletical and Trinitarian fashion, I select three. Each has to do with the indisputable fact that the Bible was written in the days of our distant ancestors.

First, the Bible is seemingly an anachronism. Where else but in churches and seminaries do people yet think that they can get the truth by reading an archaic tome? Do we do this in university philosophy departments or medical schools?

Of course, it was not always so. Once upon a time many fields of knowledge were ruled by aged textual authorities. What was science during the Middle Ages? For many it was reading Aristotle. The Philosopher said it, so people believed it. He was the scientific *logos,* the word. One accordingly spent more time expositing than experimenting. The answers were in old books. It was the same with medicine. Or rhetoric. Or whatever. The working assumption of Abelard's *Sic et Non* was that the venerable authorities are only superficially at odds: surely in the end they all agree upon everything. So all we have to do is interpret aright.

Shortly after the Renaissance, everything changed. Euclid ceased to be the last word on his subject. So too the rest of his ancient company — with one conspicuous exception. Protestant theologians and their churches decided to stick with an elderly book. The Reformers held on to the pristine Scriptures, to what they believed, in good Renaissance fashion, was the source of the river before it got polluted. Protestantism followed suit, and so our churches continued to do what nobody else did anymore — to find the first and last word in an old written authority, to settle issues with γέγραπται, "it is written."

The aberration is now more conspicuous than ever. Today's archetypal image is that of old computers — in this context "old" can mean less than five years — being constantly superseded. For us "improved" automatically goes with "new," as all the commercials prove. It is not like *Beowulf,* where the old sword is expected to be better than the new one. This does not work in our world, either for TV sets or psychology texts. To be antiquated now is to be obsolete. The soft, deceitful wiles of mass production drive us to incessant novelty — biblical studies, by the way, included. Who cares about books on the historical Jesus or Paul written a scant thirty-five years ago? Precious few. Even the guild is now filled with people who don't know their fathers, mothers, or genealogy.

So what is modernity's natural response to, its instinctive feeling about the Bible? Surely that it is aged and so passé, a book outworn. If one goes into a large bookstore, one can yet find Plato's *Dialogues* and Aristotle's *Nicomachean Ethics.* But how many other books put together at least eighty generations ago are still in print?

Now it is true that being full of years still sometimes adds prestige. A restaurant may proudly advertise that it has been serving the public for forty-five years. And maybe a few oddballs read the Egyptian *Book of the*

Dead because they think the ancients might have been on to something since forgotten. But it is no longer like the old days, when "newfangled" was always pejorative, and when the words "primitive" and "dated" were not. For most of us most of the time, age no longer in and of itself garners respect. And just as we readily ignore the elderly after we check them into the nursing home, so — sadly — we easily forget about the old books, because, after all, are there not a bunch of new ones?

In our interminably innovative world, so obsessed with so-called progress, where new knowledge as often as not does not build upon old knowledge but rather sweeps it away, it is more than counterintuitive to feel with the Renaissance theologians that our first duty is to peruse some ancient book and interpret and defend its contents — which is, after all, our Protestant heritage. When we pull out this book that is two thousand years old and say, "Look at this — all we need do is rightly divine the word of truth," we are doing what nobody else does anymore. What are the psychological ramifications of this? I suspect they are profound, and I believe that the churches ought to be doing all they can to persuade people that the past is full of treasure, that not all old things are has-beens. For those of us in the pews are, sadly, just like everybody else. Maybe we would still see Jesus, but we want him in a book just lately written, or if it is the old book, it had better be a fancy study edition with bright new covers so we can delude ourselves into feeling that our Lord is really up-to-date.

I turn now to a second predicament that the Bible finds itself in: today it is a field of specialization ruled by experts. Now those would-be experts become such by learning a lot of languages, a lot of history, and then a lot of what are called "criticisms" — textual criticism, source criticism, form criticism, redaction criticism, reader-response criticism, and all the other esoteric "isms" that have been concocted of late. That is the long, hard road to status and reward in the field, to the teaching job, to getting published, maybe even to getting fifteen minutes of fame. The consequences are serious. When there are experts, everybody else becomes an amateur. Maybe we are undoing Luther — that is, taking the book out of the hands of the many and placing it in the hands of the few, the academic priesthood. If so, how will the amateurs respond?

Consider the Jesus Seminar. What should we think if we read their press releases and their books and the reports in *Time* magazine? Many no doubt learn about the radical conclusions and can do nothing better than ignorantly dismiss the entirety of modern biblical studies. Others, more thoughtful, do not know what to believe. They wonder about the claims and the methods, but who are they to disagree with the professionals? I know confused pastors and students who feel this way. Still others say, "They have taken away my Lord, and that is just fine with me; their Jesus gets my vote."

The truth is that the sorts of issues the Jesus Seminar confronts are beyond just about everybody, including, in my opinion, us alleged experts, who bandy about our simplistic criteria of authenticity in the naïve confidence that we can play Sherlock Holmes with two-thousand-year-old religious documents and separate mundane fact from superstitious distortion. As often as not, we have, to use my favorite mixed metaphor, shaky knees with feet of clay on thin ice. But my main point here is another — namely, that the adepts disagree. In the words of Arthur C. Clarke, for each expert there is an equal and opposite expert. So what is the amateur to think? It is dismaying, if we are honest. What do we think when there is no consensus among the experts?

And there is no consensus — about Jesus or the other crucial issues. The old days of relatively easy appeal to and generalizations about the current state of scholarship are defunct. Pluralism and diversity have captured the discipline of biblical studies. Although some in the guild would disagree, I think that maybe Raymond Brown's recent introduction to the New Testament, which seeks to map the mainstream, may be the last of its kind. There is, as in the days of the judges, no king, no Rudolf Bultmann or C. H. Dodd, so all the scholars do whatever is right in their own eyes. Modernity has absconded with the consensus; the mainstream is drying up. We now have a continent of unconnected creeks. So again, what is the amateur to think?

Perhaps I am being too generous here about the public's critical senses. Many amateurs may not feel the burden that they should. Some years ago the *Washington Post* conducted a nationwide telephone poll in which people were asked about the 1975 Public Affairs Act. Over 40 percent of the respondents had strong opinions about it. Twenty-four percent said it should definitely be repealed. Nineteen percent said no, it shouldn't be repealed. Of course, there is no such thing as the 1975 Public Affairs Act. So ignorance does not always prevent people from opining. Many are going to have their suppositions about Jesus come hell or high water, just as they have their ill-informed opinions about international politics and Roswell aliens. Still, I have sometimes given a lecture or led a Bible study or taught a Sunday School class, after which someone has come up and said, "Well, that was all rather interesting, Mr. Allison, but if you really have to know so much about the Bible to understand it, I think I'll quit reading it."

How should I respond? I do not know. Maybe there is no happy response, because maybe the wise and humble thing to do, if one cannot learn enough, is to withhold judgment. But who wants to be agnostic about the New Testament or conclude that the historical Jesus is unknowable, a little patch of night in history?

One can read the Jesus Seminar's publications, but the stores also carry books purporting to demonstrate that the Jesus Seminarians are lousy historians and theophobic faddists. There are also books that represent neither the evangelicals nor the Seminar but go their own way. What should one make of it all if one reads it carefully? Everybody has some arguments. Everybody has some good arguments. What should we think?

What if, moreover, one reads Albert Schweitzer's chronicle of failed questing for Jesus and then learns from George Tyrrell how we all look down the well of history only to behold our own reflections? From one point of view, I remain fairly happy with my own book of some years ago on Jesus as a sort of millenarian prophet because I do not have a millenarian bone in my body. So I think I could be correct. But I have also written a book that turns Jesus into a sort of rabbi, whose speech was full of scriptural allusions — the intertextual Jesus. So is it just coincidence that, for me, many approaches to Scripture may abide, but the greatest of these is intertextuality?

What if one needs experts but knows how unreliable they can be? What if one has been around long enough to know that today's conclusions wither, the criticisms fade, that only the word of the text stands forever? Biblical studies has its fads just like every other field of specialization. Our theological libraries are strewn with many an Ozymandias. Who still reads the scholars who were at the top just fifty years ago?

It is useful to ask oneself what passion one would feel about, let us say, what the vote was when some radical German professors got together in 1885 and cast their red, pink, gray, and black beads to decide what Jesus really said. What if one anticipates that a century from now there will be as little interest in the no-longer-authoritative conclusions of the extinct Jesus Seminar as in my hypothetical German conclave? It is hard, upon reflection, to avoid cynicism, or not to lose respect for experts. Even if one retains respect, one may think that if the pros cannot get to the bottom of things, or if they cannot agree on what they find once they get there, then maybe it is time for more profitable pursuits.

I have recently and reluctantly come to the conclusion that biblical studies are as much a part of the postmodern carnival as anything else. The Jesus Seminar has its booth over there, with Bob Funk and Dom Crossan calling out to passersby. And then there is Luke Timothy Johnson a few booths over. Tom Wright's got his own stand, too. They are all beckoning to us. Whom do we heed?

We had better heed somebody. For the Bible is from such a different time and place that we really do require some experts. There is, to be sure, a place for the old doctrine of the perspicuity of Scripture; and I am a big believer in the power of the biblical stories as stories. My children first heard Genesis, Exodus, and the Gospels when they were learning Mother Goose. Moreover, I am not so silly as to say that, without the mediation of scholars, the Spirit cannot speak. Nor do I imagine that we need historians because we must believe only what the original authors or audiences believed, as if God would not want us to hear new things. Nonetheless, and however annoying it may be, the old book often leaves us nonplussed. Certainly it does me. How often have I wished to meet a traveler from an antique land?

Let me illustrate. The second chapter of Matthew reports that, near the time of Jesus' birth, "wise men from the East" appeared in Jerusalem and declared, "Where is he who has been born king of the Jews? For we have seen his star in the East, and have come to worship him" (2:1-2). A few verses later is this: "When they had heard the king they went their way; and lo, the star which they had seen in the East went before them, till it came to rest over the place where the child was" (2:9).

Most commentators say that the star, if there was one, was one of three things — a planetary conjunction, a comet, or a supernova, that is, a new sun. But when was the last time one of those things went ahead of somebody, or stopped over a particular place? Where is our nose for nonsense? That a light high above could precisely guide people below just does not compute. Chrysostom knew it. Bethlehem's star did not, he wrote, "remain on high and point out the place, for it was impossible for the magi so to learn it; instead it came down and performed this office. For you know that a star could not possibly mark out a spot as small as that taken up by the body of a new-born."

He is right. Incidentally, Irenaeus, Origen, Chrysologus, Leo the Great, Theophylact, Aquinas, Nicholas of Lyra, and dozens of others also tell the tale of a Tinker Bell light flying hither and yon. So what is going on here? Modernity, as so often, is in our way. The ancient conception of a star was not our conception of a star. Neither Matthew nor his premodern interpreters imagined stars to be immense, inanimate, energetic masses billions of light years away from, and thousands of times larger than, our planet. Why on earth would they think that? They lived in antiquity; and in antiquity stars were alive — they were living beings. And in Judaism stars were angels and angels were stars. Job 38:7 says, "The morning stars sang together, and all the sons of God shouted for joy." Revelation 1:20 says, "The seven stars are the angels of the seven churches." Revelation 12:4 says, "His tail swept down a third of the stars of heaven."

When one reckons with texts such as these, of which there are countless more, and then recalls that in the Bible angels are bright, that they come down from heaven to earth, and that they can serve as guides, as in the story of the Exodus, then one is going to quit thinking about modern astronomical ideas, which are, after all, modern ideas. When reading

Matthew 2, one will forget all the facts the planetarium so earnestly shares with its audiences at Christmastime and conclude that this passage tells the story of an angel. One is going to agree — if one ever happens across it, as I once did — with the old *Arabic Gospel of the Savior*. Its version of the Christmas story contains this: "Behold, magi came from the east. . . . And there were with them gifts of gold, frankincense, and myrrh. And they adored him [Jesus], and presented the gifts to him. . . . In the same hour there appeared to them an angel in the form of that star that had before guided them on their journey; and they went away, following the guidance of its light. . . ."

Sadly, the Bible has become like the new editions of Dante, or even now Shakespeare. We need footnotes written by experts all over the place, because we do not know what so much of it is saying anymore. Now as the footnotes grow longer and longer, they displace the text, which recedes further and further away from us. That the fact is sad does not undo its inevitability. Annotated study Bibles are always enlarging themselves.

But our woes do not end there. There is a third problem to grapple with. It is this: the Bible demands a certain sort of reading, a slow reading, a respectful reading, a meditative reading. It requires the sort of extended attention that puts things in the long-term memory. This is because, among other things, the canon is an intertextual wonderland. As Michael Fishbane and so many others have recently shown us, it often alludes to itself, and if one does not catch this, one has not really figured it out. Although the biblical books say much plainly, they leave much, even much of importance, unspoken. Recall Matthew's genealogy. Four women are in it, so they must mean something. But what? We are, to our frustration, never told. We are supposed to get it on our own. And that is a harbinger of things to come in this Gospel.

Matthew is, in this, typically biblical. In its own way, much of Scripture is not all that different from T. S. Eliot's poetry, in which the preferred style is allusion and implication, not the obvious. We are regularly being tacitly directed elsewhere, to the wider web of meaning. When Job gripes, "What are human beings, that you make so much of them, that you set your mind on them?" (7:17, NRSV), is he not recalling the famous Psalm 8 — "What are human beings that you are mindful of them, mortals that you care for them?" (8:4, NRSV) — and thereby inverting and mocking the liturgy? And when Luke's Jesus says that the would-be disciple who "looks at the things behind" (βλέπων εἰς τὰ ὀπίσω) is unfit for the reign of God (9:62), are we not supposed to hear, as did Tertullian, Origen, Athanasius, Bede, Albertus Magnus, Luther, and Grotius, an echo of Genesis 19, where Lot's wife loses all by "looking at the things behind" (LXX Gen. 19:17: μὴ περιβλέψῃς εἰς τὰ ὀπίσω; LXX Gen. 19:26: ἐπέβλεψεν . . . εἰς τὰ ὀπίσω)?

The holy texts are full of holes, holes waiting for informed and imaginative readers to fill them in, to make present what is absent, that being some other part of the interacting canon. Vast portions of the Bible are mnemonic triggers, set to create intertextual exchanges. But only knowledge of the tradition can find them out. As the Greeks used to say, "The gods love the cryptic and dislike the obvious."

Consider the feeding of the five thousand in Mark 6. Verse 39 says that the grass was green. This is strange. Mark's author was practically color-blind, so when he says the grass was green, we had better ask why he says it. Is the adjective the sure trace of an eyewitness, or an indication of Palestinian spring, or maybe evidence that the wilderness has begun to bring forth messianic bloom? I think not. In Mark 6 the people are like sheep without a shepherd before Jesus takes care of them. The feeding occurs beside the seashore in the evening. Everyone reclines, eats, and is satisfied. And all this happens upon the green grass. We are here given an an equation to be solved: shepherd + green grass + having no lack + being beside the water + reclining = the Twenty-third Psalm. "The Lord is my shepherd, I shall not want. . . ." But how many modern readers see this?

Sometimes we do not get the joke. We can equally miss the omnipresent allusions in Scripture. One reason is that our memorization skills are languishing. Plato saw it coming. He said that putting more and more on paper would become a substitute for memory. He was right. I fre-

quently do not know something, only where to find it. I have memorized
the lesser thing. Aldous Huxley had a set of the *Encyclopedia Britannica*
put into the back of his car, so he could look things up wherever he went.
He carried his memory in his trunk. Much of mine is now on disk.

Ours is the age that damned "rote memorization." My children, who
can recite Blake, Shelley, and Keats, are anomalies for it. Our memories
for print have become enfeebled. So when we read the Bible, we usually
are not bringing the requisite intertexts along with us. We are not reading between the lines, which means we are not reading rightly.

Another part of the problem is that today we try *not* to read slowly.
Speed-reading is one of the twentieth century's dubious contributions
to the annals of education. Even when we do learn to read well, we are
encouraged, for no good reason, to do so rapidly. But authentic reading
should be like gazing at the stars: it demands that we stop. It should be
like staring at a fire: it occasions reflection. It should be like bird-
watching: it requires patience. We think reading swiftly is a sign of intelligence. Is it not just silly?

The ancients who read almost always read out loud — like the Ethio-
pian eunuch in Acts — and most people could not read at all and so only
heard texts. That required slowing down, as did the fact that the old texts
were all written in continuous script, without divisions or punctuation
between words or sentences or paragraphs. One of the first references to
somebody reading silently comes from the fourth century A.D. It was a
marvel that merited mention (Augustine had seen Ambrose do it). Now
we all know that recitation makes for better memory than sight-reading
alone. Conversely, not reciting or hearing something makes it less memorable. By reading silently, then, we have made books, including the Bible,
less memorable.

We fail to catch scriptural allusions not because most of the Bible is
like Heraclitus, who wrote obscurely so that only the highbrows would
read him. The problem is, rather, us. Let me draw an analogy. Much of
the power of Martin Luther King Jr.'s widely appreciated rhetoric came
from his expectation that his hearers would perceive the implicit. When
he gave his famous "I Have a Dream" speech, he expected his audience to
hear in his first words, "Five score years ago," an echo of the first words

of the Gettysburg Address. It was a way of saying, "My cause is the completion of what Lincoln began." When King spoke of "this sweltering summer of the Negro's discontent," he was alluding to the opening lines of Shakespeare's *Richard III* — "Now is the winter of our discontent/Made glorious summer by this sun of York" — and thereby telling the whites in his audience, "You cannot ignore me. I know your European tradition as well as you do." When he said, "We will not be satisfied until justice rolls down like waters and righteousness like a mighty stream," surely he believed that his hearers would know this was from the Bible (Amos 5:24). King was asserting, "God is on my side."

Now I do not think that King expected too much of his audience. In his time and place, the implied connections were not occluded. But I know from disconcerting experience that, in the present day and age, most college students of whatever ethnic group reading King's speech are literarily challenged. They see only the conspicuous. For them the many tacit references, which add so much meaning, are beyond subtle: they are not there at all. As the culture changes, what was once obvious becomes invisible. Now we, the forgetful, need footnotes: "The Gettysburg Address was delivered by Abraham Lincoln on the occasion of. . . . Its opening words are. . . ."

We may still, thank God, comprehend the plain words of the Bible. But notwithstanding all good faith and goodwill, if that is all we are comprehending, we are not reading well. If microscopes reveal our native blindness to many worlds, critical study and careful rereading inform us that the Bible holds a thousand hidden pictures, and seeing, we do not see: "I can see people, but they look like trees, walking" (Mark 8:24, NRSV).

Josephus said that first-century Jews had a "thorough and accurate knowledge" of the Scriptures. Maybe he was being a bit rhetorical. But he thought he could get away with it, and the New Testament writers — most if not all of them Jews — do not refute him. But could anyone today get away with claiming that mainline Protestants have a thorough and accurate knowledge of the Bible? We could put our congregations to the proof by letting them sing the once-famous lines from Toplady's old hymn "Rock of Ages":

Rock of Ages, cleft for me,
Let me hide myself in Thee!
Let the water and the blood,
From Thy riven side which flowed,
Be of sin the double cure . . .

Would they remember John 19, where water and blood flow from Christ's riven side? Surely many of them would. Would they recall Exodus 17 and the water from the rock? One doubts it. Would they recollect 1 Corinthians 10, which says "and the rock was Christ"? Of course not. And would their memories retrieve Exodus 33, where Moses hides himself in the cleft of a rock? It seems scarcely possible. We have dropped "Onward, Christian Soldiers" from the hymnbooks. "Onward, Christian Readers" is never going to make it in. When Jesus asked, "Have you not read?" he expected an affirmative answer. Things change.

The situation, it seems to me, is truly dire. Maybe we shall never have a new birth of Bible reading, and our book shall indeed perish from the earth. I am certainly not holding my breath for our literary convalescence. If reading the Bible has lost its taste, how will its flavor be restored?

One might object that my reflections come from some sort of pessimistic Gnostic. Surely the salvation of the world does not depend upon reading skills. Coleridge did not write that they "prayeth best who readeth best"; and would it not be going too far to say that the Lord knows the way of the literate, but the way of the illiterate will perish? Surely neither reading nor not reading counts for anything, but a new creation, which the Spirit that blows where it wills can work without pages.

Maybe so. But what if the Spirit prefers to move over the face of the text? That is my nostalgic opinion. For the Spirit must know that reading much and reading rightly invigorate our imaginations, and that not reading much and not reading rightly dull them; and with atrophied imaginations we have run and will run in vain. We need to grow in wisdom and stature and in favor with God and the text. My own version of Christian Darwinism holds that it is the fittest readers who will survive.

Some, less bookish than myself, believe that form is a matter of indifference. All we need, then, is an information transfer from one medium to another. Now I have not yet run across the proposal that we lay out the Bible in PowerPoint, but I do know those who think that we can make things better by transmuting Scripture into an audiovisual experience. That would secure the popular favor, would it not? On this matter I sit in the seat of scoffers, for Marshall McLuhan was right: form matters; all media are not equal. Meaning is like water: it is shaped by the container it fills. Mel Gibson's *Passion of the Christ,* whatever else one may say about it, is no equivalent to the four written passion narratives. Even the best films can only reach so far. How could the movies ever do Leviticus or Proverbs or Romans or Hebrews? Surely the one who sits in the heavens laughs. "Bible," after all, means "book."

The church has a great stake in literacy, because people who do not love to read are not likely to wrestle until the breaking of the day with the Bible and the parasitic literature now needed to understand it. But how can the church promote a love of reading in general and of the Scriptures in particular? How can the book that we moderns have rejected become again marvelous in our eyes? I wish I had an answer.

Does anyone remember the famous British bookaholic Richard Heber, who so coveted books? For him, to see a book was to desire it. He stuffed the rooms, the cupboards, the corridors of eight large houses with his collection. But has not Heber's disease, which was once common enough to have a name, "bibliomania," been almost eradicated? When I now walk into my local public library, I see more people at the computer terminals than in the stacks. In the age of ADD and Nintendo, the world is filled with more and more people just like my hairdresser. She wants to read and tries to read, but she just cannot do it. Five minutes after opening a book, she is surfing the Internet.

I know nothing that offsets my depressing and unedifying analysis of our current situation. I think we are in trouble, and I honestly expect things to get worse. So all I can do, at the end of this chapter, is all too briefly offer a sort of personal testimony and explain why I have not myself given up on reading the Bible.

From a purely human point of view, the Bible has for me always been akin to reading one of the great detective novels, *Trent's Last Case* or *The Three Coffins*. Early on I discovered the allusive nature of Scripture, and it has kept me in suspense ever since. I remember how animated I became, so many years ago now, when I first espied Matthew's new Moses typology, when I first saw that the series of events in Matthew 1-7 recapitulates the story of Moses and the Exodus from Egypt:

1. Israel's deliverer is born.
2. A wicked king sits upon the throne.
3. That king slaughters Jewish infants.
4. The hero's years after infancy go unrecounted.
5. He passes through the waters.
6. He goes into the desert.
7. He stays there for a period of time marked by forty units.
8. Temptation comes in the form of hunger and idolatry.
9. The deliverer goes up on a mountain.
10. We learn the commandments.

Discovering the pattern, scrutinizing the details, finding other Moses typologies in ancient literature, and investigating how much of Matthew's scheme readers across the centuries have perceived brought great joy, the joy of discovery. (And it was, by the way, discovery. Matthew never once condescended to say that Jesus is like Moses. He knew that the explicit is soon enough tedious, that the allusion fights fatigue. Meaning is infolded not to obscure but to improve communication: allusions give the imagination more to do and so heighten attention.)

My becoming aware of the new Moses motif stands for a host of experiences. In my case, then, distance from the Bible has made it more fascinating: a new planet is always swimming into my ken. I am ever intrigued because I am always just beginning to see something that the ancients knew but that we have forgotten. And the canon is sufficiently dense that, God willing, I still have three or more decades of exploration ahead. And after Saint Peter lets me into the world to come, I hope Rabbi Judah the Prince lets me sit in the dust at the feet of the Tanna'im as words of Torah pass between them. It would be heaven to be with the dogs that eat of the crumbs falling from that table.

But of course the Bible is so much more than a great puzzle book whose secrets can sometimes be unearthed by the reductionistic historical criticism with which, for good or ill, I was indoctrinated in my youth. The inexplicable divine mystery still speaks through the old pages and through my hermeneutical confusion; and in the end I must pursue the book because it has always pursued me. It has made me feel like a worm and no man, and it has made me sing the song of Simeon. It has made known my transgressions so that they are ever before me, and it has freed me from my past so that I am free indeed. It has so shaped my intellect that, even when I do not end with it, I always begin with it. And what little good deed doing I have done has come from memory of the Good Samaritan and of the Son of Man's words to the sheep and the goats.

I have come to live and move and have my being in the Bible, as also in the Jewish Halakha and Haggadah that illuminate it, and in the history of its interpretation, and in the Christian traditions it has brought forth. I want this book read to me on my deathbed. Despite my modernity and my cynical nature, despite my dissection of it and my quarrels with it, the Bible remains profitable for teaching, for correction, and for training in righteousness. It comforts. It inspires. It commands. When I push its pages apart, I lay my finger on God's heart. I hate to see people not reading it.

CHAPTER 5

Saints and Heroes

When you see an individual of the highest caliber, give thought to attaining that person's stature. When you see one who is not, go home and conduct a self-examination.

Confucius

Be imitators of me, as I am of Christ.

Saint Paul, 1 Corinthians 11:1

Not in mere words only did this teacher go over the truths concerning the virtues with us; but he incited us much more to the practice of virtue, and stimulated us by the deeds he did more than by the doctrines he taught.

Gregory Thaumaturgus, on Origen

The Christian and the hero are inseparable.

Samuel Johnson

Matthew, Mark, Luke, and John: the Four Gospels. I like to think, having toiled so many years writing a commentary on the first of these, that it is in some ways the most important, and that its initial placement intimates this. The First Gospel has, without doubt, ruled Christian ethics, for which the Sermon on the Mount, not found in the other three Gospels, is the quintessence and conscience. It has, further, dominated the liturgies. The churches — Eastern Orthodox, Roman Catholic, Protestant — recite the Lord's Prayer as it appears in Matthew, not Luke's rather different version.

Whether my personal preference can be turned into an argument is, however, of no account here, only that Matthew is, by every measure, a most important book, and I should like to ask, What sort of a book is it? What, as the literary critics might inquire, is its *genre*?

The Gospel purports to record Jesus' ancestry and infancy, his words and deeds, his death and resurrection, and it sets these things forth in chronological order: the birth is narrated before the ministry, the ministry before the death, and the death before the resurrection. Matthew accordingly appears to be a sort of biography. There are, to be sure, many gaps in the story — What did Jesus do before John the Baptist appeared? — gaps that puzzle modern readers, who equate biography with comprehensive review. Matthew is, to our frustration and incredulity, only the very partial telling of a life. But this should not blind us to the obvious, especially as many Graeco-Roman biographies were, from our point of view, fragmentary. Matthew is the story, however incomplete, of what Jesus said and did, and of what was done to him.

The fact raises an instructive issue, for there were many types of literature — nonbiographical types of literature — available to early Christians wanting to communicate their faith. There was the epistle or letter (Paul wrote such). There was the apocalypse, or tract about the latter days (Revelation being an example). There was the collection of sayings (one thinks of the Old Testament's book of Proverbs, or of the famous Gospel of Thomas, discovered in the 1940s). And there was the religious apology, or defense of the faith (the second-century church father Justin Martyr wrote apologies). But Matthew is not exactly any of these. My question is, Why? Why a book about a man's life, a book of words and deeds and events?

The import of the question can be appreciated only when Matthew's comparatively brief work is set over against the great literary treasure of rabbinic Judaism in all its forms. In the rabbinic sources there are multitudinous stories about rabbis but not one sustained life; there is report upon report of what Rabbi X or Rabbi Y said, usually in the name of Rabbi Z, but there are no biographies. More than this, particular sages are only rarely organizing foci in rabbinic literature. Not often does the Talmud run together several sayings from one master.

Biography was also foreign to the Essenes, the Jewish sectarians who wrote and hid the Dead Sea Scrolls. The Scrolls do, on several occasions, refer to a so-called Teacher of Righteousness, a mysterious figure of foundational importance. Sadly, however, it is impossible to say much about him. Despite his obvious significance, his followers did not, from what we can gather, pass on many traditions about him. He never found a biographer. Nor did any of the Essenes who came after him.

Comparison with the works of rabbinic Judaism and the Dead Sea Scrolls discloses that Matthew's biographical character should not be taken for granted. Rather, that character requires an explanation. We, however, have before us a text that does not supply such an explanation; that is, the text offers no reason for its literary form, so of its express purpose we cannot speak. Still, we may observe — and here I appeal to the self-evident — that the substance of the author's faith, unlike the faith of the rabbis, was neither a dogmatic system nor a legal code but instead a human being whose life was, in outline and in detail, uniquely significant and therefore demanding of record. Jesus himself says, in chapter 11, "Learn of me." So is it really surprising that we have our Gospel? Matthew's Christology, his understanding of Jesus Christ, certainly encouraged and perhaps even demanded biography.

That, however, does not tell us everything. Biography was also surely encouraged by the circumstance that many of the sayings passed down under Jesus' name were incomplete apart from a narrative or story. Imagine what might be the meaning, without any setting, of "Leave the dead to bury their own dead" (8:22 — that one is hard enough even with a context), or of "Go nowhere among the Gentiles" (10:5), or of "Take no gold, nor silver, nor copper in your belts" (10:9).

These and many other sayings in Matthew just do not work as proverbs or general maxims. Devoid of a context within a story, the utterances become either meaningless or misleading. Our Gospel, with its biographical form, implicitly recognizes this fact: the tradition about Jesus was not a collection of self-authenticating proverbs or timeless truths. It was rather the reflection of a historical encounter. Much of it was, so to speak, naked without a narrative. Content demanded context, word required story, speech demanded biography.

I should like to suggest, however, that yet another factor augmented the biographical impulse that gave birth to the First Gospel. I begin with this observation: the more history one learns, the less it seems that any period, of however short or long a duration, has been free of crisis. All times are out of joint. Historical stability appears to be a fiction, for something new is always confronting the status quo, and people are always anxious about what the future holds. Nonetheless, the idea of a historical crisis retains substance, for some periods are indeed more racked by strife and anxiety than others. And such was the first century, at least in Palestine, the cradle of Christianity. That epoch saw Jews revolt against Rome and lose their temple; it witnessed the birth of the Zealots and the death of the Essenes; and it saw the production of several lengthy apocalypses, a sure sign of profound dissatisfaction.

What does all this have to do with Matthew? Perhaps much, for historians have observed that the production of biographies has been encouraged by periods of social crisis. Reflection offers an explanation: whenever a social crisis results, as it so often does, in fragmentation — that is, whenever social conflict is sufficiently severe so as to issue in the formation of a new social unit, as happened at the birth of the church when Christians started their own religious movement — two things happen: first, old norms and authorities are jettisoned; and second, new norms and authorities are inevitably substituted.

This matters to us because such norms and authorities are always most persuasively presented when embodied in examples. New fashions must first be modeled; somebody must first wear the clothes. Certainly this happened at the Protestant Reformation. The break with Roman Catholicism brought many into a new world, with new standards of belief and behavior. In response, new biographies were produced, biographies exhibiting the new beliefs and recommended behavior. The Reformation replaced the traditional constellation of Catholic saints with its own lights, the new Protestant heroes. Popular biography, especially martyrology, flourished. (John Foxe published his famous *Acts and Monuments of Matters Happening in the Church,* popularly known as *Foxe's Book of Martyrs,* in 1563.)

Something similar happened as a result of the social fragmentation that engendered early Christianity. The first Christians, whether Jew or Gentile, had made a change of allegiance. They had come to new beliefs and new ways of behaving. Accordingly, new models were needed. And Jesus himself, through the promulgation of the tradition about him, became the new model *par excellence.* This fact has been insufficiently appreciated in many quarters, in part because there has been, since Martin Luther, a theological reaction against an unimaginative and literalistic "imitation of Christ" (such as that exhibited by Francis of Assisi), in part because the notion of the emulation of Jesus has been condemned by certain theologians as a "purely human effort," one which, in any event, cannot be achieved, and in part because many have been anxious to preserve Jesus' unique status as a savior whose accomplishments for others cannot be duplicated. But such issues did not, as far as I can see, concern the first Christians. Further, Matthew wrote long before the later Christological debates, wrote when it was still possible to think of Jesus as a genuine human being (whatever else Christians believed him to be) and thus as a genuine ethical model; and Matthew, like other early believers, including Paul and Origen, thought of Jesus as a model to be emulated.

This is why, despite the general silence of the commentators, there is in the First Gospel a multitude of obvious and significant connections between Jesus' words and his deeds, so that Jesus becomes the great illustrator of his injunctions. If Jesus indirectly exhorted others to be meek ("Blessed are the meek," 5:5), he himself was such ("I am meek and lowly in heart," 11:29, KJV; cf. 21:5). If he enjoined mercy ("Blessed are the merciful," 5:7), he himself was merciful ("Have mercy on us, Son of David," 9:27; cf. 15:22; 20:30). If he congratulated those oppressed for God's cause ("Blessed are those who are persecuted for righteousness' sake," 5:10), he himself suffered and died innocently ("And he [Pilate] said, '. . . what evil has he done?'" 27:23). Jesus further demanded faithfulness to the law of Moses ("Think not that I have come to abolish the law and the prophets," 5:17-20) and faithfully kept that law during his ministry ("Show yourself to the priest, and offer the gift that Moses commanded," 8:4; cf. 12:1-8, 9-14; 15:1-20). He recommended self-denial in the face of evil ("If anyone strikes you on the right cheek, turn to him the other also," 5:39) and did not resist the evils done to him ("They spat in his face, and struck him; and some slapped him," 26:67; cf. 27:30). He called for private prayer ("When you pray, go into your room and shut the door and pray to your Father who is in secret," 6:6) and subsequently prayed in private ("He went up on the mountain by himself to pray," 14:23). Moreover, Jesus advised his followers to use certain words in prayer ("Thy kingdom come, thy will be done," 6:10), and he used those very words in Gethsemane ("If this cannot pass unless I drink it, thy will be done," 26:42). He rejected the service of mammon ("Do not lay up for yourselves treasures on earth," 6:19), and he lived without concern for money ("The Son of man has nowhere to lay his head," 8:20). One last example: Jesus commanded those who would come after him to deny themselves and take up crosses (16:24), and he did so himself, both figuratively and literally. One could go on and on in this vein, citing instances of Jesus animating his speech. (It would be helpful if someone would supply us with a catalogue: I do not know of any).

Consider also that Matthew went out of his way to demonstrate that the Twelve emulated their Lord in numerous particulars. Chapter 10 alone offers the following parallels:

The disciples	Jesus
They are to "heal every disease and every infirmity" (10:1)	He heals every disease and every infirmity (4:23)
They are to preach that "the kingdom of heaven is at hand" (10:7)	He preaches that "the kingdom of heaven is at hand" (4:17)
They are to cast out demons (10:8)	He casts out demons (4:24; 9:32-33, etc.)
They are to heal lepers (10:8)	He heals lepers (11:5)

They are to raise the dead (10:8)	He raises the dead (11:5)
They are not to go to the Samaritans (10:5)	He does not go to the Samaritans (15:24)
They will be handed over to sanhedrins (10:17)	Jesus is handed over to the Sanhedrin (26:57-68)
They will be "dragged before governors" (10:18)	Jesus is taken before the governor (27:1-2, 11-26)
They will be called the servants of Beelzebul (10:25)	Jesus is called the servant of Beelzebul (9:34; 10:25)

What is implied by these correlations? If the disciples imitated Jesus, the thought that others should follow their lead and do likewise lies very near to hand. On the moral level at least, our Gospel encourages its readers to identify closely not only with the disciples but also with the main character, whom the text presents as, in the words of Hebrews, "the pioneer and perfecter of our faith" (12:2). If Aristotle nominated the "good man" as the "canon" or rule in ethics, Matthew considered Jesus the "canon" of Christian morality: the Messiah went infallibly right. Jesus demanded the perfect imitation of God ("You, therefore, must be perfect, as your heavenly Father is perfect," Matt. 5:48), and he himself was the outstanding instance of such perfect imitation.

André Maurois wrote that "biography is a type of literature which, more than any other, touches close upon morality." This must be true. Prior to recent times, in which biographers have been so preoccupied with information, entertainment, and psychology, biography has usually, to a greater or a lesser degree, enshrined clear moral aims: books about individuals have commended or condemned them and their behavior. One thinks, for instance, of the proliferation of biographies among the early Puritans, with their omnipresent exhortations designed to prevent or remedy character defects, or of the "moralizing" — the word now suffers ill repute — in the one-time well-read biographies of Samuel Smiles, such as *Lives of the Engineers* and *Men of Invention and Industry,* the sorts of books not much written after Lytton Strachey's *Eminent Victorians* (1918). Plutarch's *Lives* (which so much influenced nineteenth-century biography), Petrarch's biographies, and the Roman Catholic and Eastern Orthodox legends of the saints also come instantly to mind, as does much else. Athanasius wrote his famous *Life of Anthony* in part to supply "an ideal pattern" for others desirous to "emulate his [Anthony's] resolution." The opinion of Samuel Johnson has no doubt been implicitly held by many: "No species of writing seems more worthy of cultivation than biography since none can be more delightful or more useful, none can more certainly enchain the heart by irresistible interest, or more widely diffuse instruction of every diversity of condition." Thomas Carlyle put it succinctly: "Biography is almost the one thing needful."

One recalls the old maxim that "the greatest influence upon our conduct is the conduct of others." From this undoubted truth of psychology, that we emulate those who appear before us, it follows that if one wishes to shape behavior and impact morality, one will be well advised to put forward what Milton termed "the salutary influence of example." Words will not suffice. One must employ sight as well as sound. That is why Hebrews 11 conjures in the mind's eye visions of well-known heroes and their deeds, and also why the Talmud observes that the Torah is learned not just through study of a book but also through sitting at the feet of the rabbi: see what the master does and go and do likewise.

Smiles wrote, "Example is one of the most potent of instructors, though it teaches without a tongue. It is the practical school of mankind, working by action, which is always more forcible than words." This declaration is nothing other than a wordy, Victorian version of the old, concise Latin proverb: Example is better than precept. As Seneca noted, "The way is long if one follows precept, but short and helpful if one follows patterns." The sentiment is crucial for understanding Matthew. For the book's passionate moral preoccupation, apparent above all in the Sermon on the Mount, could not have been better served than by a story in which the crucial moral imperatives are imaginatively and convincingly incarnated. And exactly this is supplied. Matthew, to quote Clement of Alexandria, offers two types of teaching, "that which assumes the form of counselling to obedience, and that which is presented in the form of example."

When Eduard Thurneysen forwarded his Christological interpretation of the Sermon on the Mount, according to which this last is a self-portrait, he hit a mass of truth. The First Evangelist did seek to show that Jesus embodied his speech, that the Lord lived as he spoke and spoke as he lived. Further, I am certain that Matthew would have concurred with Maximus the Confessor: "Those who love Christ thoroughly imitate him as much as they can." In sum, then, a pedagogical wisdom, which knew that the good illustration is the best sermon, produced Matthew's little biography of Jesus, in which the congruent words and deeds become exemplary imperatives.

All that I have said so far should be obvious. Indeed, I am tempted to think my words banalities. Yet, if so, they are necessary banalities, for we live at a time when the moral model or hero plays little role in learning. The diminishment is of course a symptom of something much larger, that being the slow evaporation of our traditional ethical wisdom, an evaporation whose explanation requires a long history lesson which herein can only be writ small.

In the sixteenth century, following the pessimism fostered by three centuries of plague, Luther, Calvin, and the Jansenists so depredated human nature as to make morality seem of little account. An irrational grace swallowed up the significance of human effort. Then, in the seventeenth and eighteenth centuries, the Enlightenment thinkers, having witnessed the excesses of religious passion in the wars of religion, promoted a political tolerance (the Toleration Act passed in 1689) which grew into the sort of liberal individualism later celebrated by John Dewey: the self is an isolated source of value whose moral *telos* is defined not by conventional social roles but by autonomous reason. Thereafter, the Romantic movement and Rousseau handed down, in opposition to both Aristotle and Christianity, the doctrine of natural goodness: if uncorrupted by a bad environment, virtue will naturally take root and blossom of its own accord.

In the nineteenth century, the retreat of Christianity turned heaven, theretofore a certain conviction, into an uncertain hope. Victorian England found reassurance in seances (which were taken with sufficient seriousness to have been studied by the likes of Henry Sidgwick and Sir William Crookes). And hell, when believed in at all, came less to be feared than tuberculosis. It indeed soon became a metaphor (Blake and Shelley used it of London); and Dante's *Inferno* was read as though it were Greek mythology. While all but a very few were uncertain that morality could manage entirely without religion, moral imperatives were no longer bound to everlasting rewards or eternal punishments. (Witness the advent and influence of English utilitarianism, based upon this-worldly measurements.)

In the twentieth and twenty-first centuries, the explosion of knowledge, international travel, and the integration of cultures in the Western urban centers have generated a pluralism that requires the tolerance of no absolutes. The once-radical relativism of Margaret Mead's *Coming of Age in Samoa* (1920) is now the instinctive wisdom.

Alienation from earlier ways of thinking about right and wrong has, in our time, mated with an uncritical faith in the possibilities of formal education (a strange faith with its own complex history). Together they have begotten the habit of reducing moral education to barren verbal discourse. We now think, or perhaps I should say feel, that people can be guided, their behavior altered, through classroom instruction, that direction can be found in discussion of hypothetical situations ("values clarification"), or in rational dialogue (Lawrence Kohlberg's "moral reasoning"), or even in slogans ("Just say NO"). But people are not computers whose output is determined by programs. Words and ideas are not our sovereigns. We are animals, which means creatures of habit; and our habits are formed by the repeated imitation of others of the same species, others close to hand. This is why family life is inescapably formative: behavior is molded most by observation. Here the behaviorists were right: "imprinting" is fundamental: the eyes paint the soul. Example is better than precept because example is stronger than precept. As experience proves, the catechism communicates nothing if not incarnated in a community or a person.

The attempt to order behavior primarily through information and verbal imperatives is deficient not only because it underestimates the overwhelming impulse to imitate what is seen with the physical eyes, but also because it overlooks the captivating power of what can be seen with the inner eyes. Jesus left us not so much with a new list of imperatives as with, first, a host of novel images — putting a light under a bushel, plucking out one's right eye, building a house on the sand — and, second, a series of memorable stories — the good Samaritan, the rich man and Lazarus, the sower who went out to sow. He well knew that we are piloted by imagination, and, moreover, that this miraculous faculty allows us to live even in fictional stories, which can shape us almost as powerfully as persons and events in the sensual world. As Aristotle observed, "The same passion and movement that is caused by all the external senses upon the soul is likewise caused by the imagination alone," and "In the thinking soul, images play the part of precepts." This explains why we are shaped by the heroes who inhabit our narratives just as we are shaped by family and friends. That is the wisdom of Jesus' teaching. It is also the wisdom of Matthew's Gospel as well as of most traditional biography. Example is, to repeat, stronger than precept.

But what happens when a culture's stock of moral heroes dwindles? What ensues when the imagination loses Odysseus and Joan of Arc, when it does not much engage the time-tested heroic tales that unforgettably display courage, honesty, faithfulness — the priceless things Kohlberg inanely disparages as belonging to "the old bag of virtues"? Inevitably the fires of the mind find fuel elsewhere. This is what has happened to us.

The eyes of human hearts must always look up; and today, regrettably, they look up at countless celebrities, who now occupy us as heroes occupied those before us. But, as Daniel Boorstin observed in *The Image*, there has not been a substitution of equivalencies; for while both the hero and the celebrity are of wide reputation, and while perhaps they both assuage the same messianic longing, they are otherwise very different.

To generalize: heroes are known for accomplishments, their fame being a consequence of greatness. Celebrities, who need be neither good nor bad but only famous, are known for being well-known; that is, they are products of marketing. Heroes are most often dead, their reputations enhanced by time's passage. Celebrities are contemporaries (which is why we want Elvis alive); they often find themselves famous in an instant. Heroes gain their reputations in war or politics, or by thinking new thoughts, or (as in the Bible) by being remade by God. Celebrities usually belong to the world of entertainment. Heroes are scarce, their value accordingly high. Celebrities are numerous, their value accordingly low. Heroes enjoy long-lasting fame. Celebrities know that fame is a passing cloud. (This last fact is illustrated by the ongoing publication of the popular series "Whatever became of . . . ?" The celebrity is, most often, a one-night stand.)

The distinctions enumerated by Boorstin may be illuminated by comparing one hero with one celebrity. I choose to juxtapose Alexander the Great and (for no particular reason) Ms. Jane Russell. The former became famous through a military campaign of massive and unprecedented scale, a campaign executed with strategic brilliance, dogged persistence, and great daring. Its extreme hardships cost Alexander his life. Moreover, the early sources reveal a fascinating character full of complexities and contradictions. Although Alexander was tutored by Aristotle himself, he was hardly the embodiment of the golden mean. All too often, despite his iron will, he was a man of hot impatience. Once, upset by the failure of his men to scale the wall of a besieged Indian citadel, he himself picked up a ladder and climbed to the top; then, like a Viking berserker, he jumped into the throng below, to fight the terrified citizens all by himself. Further, although he could be unjustly cruel to those nearest him, he is perhaps, according to W. W. Tarn, "the only character in Greek public life who is ever recorded to have felt pity" (pity was not a virtue to the Greeks); and whereas Alexander was reared as a Greek and took his civilization to the barbarian world, he nevertheless, anticipating the Stoics and Paul, developed a cosmopolitan outlook. Groping toward some vision of "the brotherhood of mankind," he wanted to fuse the races. He took the first step himself by marrying Roxana, a Bactrian. By all accounts he was extraordinary, and his eventful life, which remapped the world, is full of instruction and unforgettable episodes. He dreamed greatly and acted greatly — and all before dying at thirty-three.

The triumph of Alexander was not even vanquished by death, for time only added to his reputation. One understands why some, as Plutarch reports, believed Alexander to have been begotten by a god, why Julius Caesar took him as a model, why *The Greek Alexander Romance* is not a book of sober history but a collection of myths and legends, why the Abyssinian Christians canonized the man, and why the Bedouin took Napoleon to be Alexander come again.

And what of Ms. Jane Russell? Her status as a celebrity is established by her faded fame: those under a certain age know her not. But in her day, in the 1950s, she was a "star." Her face and figure were celebrated, her movies successful. Why? Only because the publicity for her was effective (Howard Hughes put up the money). It is not disrespectful to observe that Ms. Russell did nothing extraordinary. Unlike Alexander, she neither thought nor did anything new, never accomplished anything unique or of lasting consequence. A short list of movies exhausts her achievements (rightly ignored by the latest *Britannica*); and apart from her handsome countenance, buxom torso, and average acting abilities, one has difficulty naming either her virtues or her vices (although these last must, at one time, have been rumored). And yet the fantastic fact is that, even now, many Americans know far more about Ms. Jane Russell than about Alexander the Great.

The one fantastic fact is not lonely; it rather enjoys a crowd of fantastic facts. Almost all of us know a hundredfold more about a thousand celebrities than about old Alexander. That this is foolish and perverse poverty I need not contend. What would one think of a person who argued otherwise? Obviously our hearts and memories are in the wrong place. Never before, I must believe, have so many known so much of so little importance. Common knowledge about Marilyn Monroe, Elvis Presley, and their ilk is the new social cohesion (which partly explains why we are falling apart). But no more than Jane Russell did Marilyn or Elvis — we naturally use their first names, as we do with Jesus and Paul — do anything we really need know about. They simply entertained us from time to time; and then they walked offstage and into our nostalgia.

If this unhappy fiasco — our peculiar absorption with celebrities — cannot be cheered, we can, following Boorstin's lead, at least guess its sources. The democratic ideal, or rather what it has come to mean, has contributed greatly. "All men are created equal." While originally a statement of equality of rights, the meaning has mutated into equality of condition. A century and a half ago, Alexis de Tocqueville fretted that Christian morality was being supplanted by a new social morality of egalitarianism. He wrote, "The revolutions that displaced the old European ruling class, the general extension of wealth and education which has made individuals more and more alike have given an immense and unexpected impetus to the principle of equality, which Christianity has established in the spiritual rather than in the tangible material sphere."

Tocqueville's observation was accurate, and in our time equality has so ballooned that many even imagine all to be somehow morally equal, imagine that no one person is better than any other. On this view (which strangely resembles the Reformed notion that all sinners are equally sinful), moral superiority is a fiction, and moral heroes have no place. "Contempt for the heroic is only an extension of the perversion of the democratic principle that denies greatness and wants everyone to feel comfortable in his skin without having to suffer unpleasant consequences." The quoted words are from Allan Bloom, who reports that, in his experience, American college students, when asked to name their heroes, go mute.

In addition to the problems due to our ideology of equality, the acids of modern historiography have become increasingly corrosive. We now know that many of the stories so fondly repeated about heroes are legendary, untrue. No one has eluded criticism. The edifying tales about presidents have fared no better than the lives of the saints. Saint Catherine, we learn today, did not undergo a martyrdom because she did not even exist (and so has left the Roman Catholic calendar); and George Washington, whether honest or not, did not chop down the cherry tree. The earlier hagiography of Smiles, moreover, has transmuted itself into brutal works that leave none unsullied. Strachey's account of Florence

Nightingale, Van Wyck Brooks's *Mark Twain,* Richard Grenier's *The Gandhi Nobody Knows,* and Morton Smith's *Jesus the Magician* are all representative. Oscar Wilde remarked that modern biography "adds to death a new terror." The romantic has been crucified by the critical and scientific. Carl Sandburg's *Lincoln* no longer engenders inspiration but prompts condescending smiles. The historical-critical method has seemingly established the truth of the scriptural assessment: "There is not one that is righteous, no, not one."

We are additionally suspicious of the former heroes because, as willing disciples of the three John the Baptists of modernity — Darwin, Marx, and Freud — we regard human beings as "Mere puppets . . . who come and go / At the bidding of vast formless things / That shift the scenery to and fro" (Poe).

Anxious to assume less responsibility, we have come to believe ourselves the yielding clay of biology, economics, and childhood experience. Were not Leonardo da Vinci's unbounded creativity and addiction to research midwifed by anxious curiosity about an absent father and then brought to maturation by a sublimated homosexuality (Freud)? Should we not trace Luther's rebellious spirit and his wrestling with God to a neurosis born of ill-health, brutal parents, and an ineradicable melancholy (Erik Erikson)? Were not the grand and high-minded ideas of the Founding Fathers largely fancy dress for economic self-interest (Charles Beard)? The hermeneutics of suspicion reigns, and heroic deeds are regularly deciphered as symbolic fantasies. If appearances are deceiving, that is our opportunity to humble the exalted. But heroes interpreted in nonheroic terms are heroes no more.

(I must add that to interpret ourselves as marionettes alters our understanding not only of heroes and their virtues but also of villains and their vices. If responsibility lies not within souls but without them, in extraneous and uncontrollable factors, in DNA, in early family life, and in social and political circumstances, then evil is only the effect of misfortune, and sin collective culpability. One understands why there are those among us who believe not only that Hitler was mainly called forth by economic circumstances, but also that the German people only succumbed to the inevitable, and that therefore no one was really responsible. "Ethics without virtue," to use Christina Sommers's phrase, means ethics without vice. When the hero leaves, so does the villain. The fact is so obvious that college courses in applied ethics are today rarely about virtue but instead about institutional policies. How far should we go with gene splicing? Is capital punishment a good thing? When should the doctors deliver up the patient to death? In this way public policy swallows up ethics, and collectivism excuses us all. Maybe Lucifer fell because the ground was wet.)

Our inclination to demythologize must owe something to the modern idea of progress. It is true that the ancients knew of the progress of knowledge and hoped for the advance of human nature. Xenophanes wrote that "the gods did not reveal all things from the beginning, but men through their own searches find in the course of time that which is better," and Augustine praised "progress in agriculture and navigation." It is also true that the idea of universal progress is no longer (if it ever was) an unquestioned dogma: Nietzsche and Spengler have their disciples, and Orwell's *1984* is (or at least used to be) a staple of high school and college curricula. Still, technology's marvelous inventions for greater health and comfort make it hard to abandon the notion that the future is a better place, that fifty or maybe five hundred years will make all right with the world. Do we not still believe that, in the end, "Star Trek" is our manifest destiny? I am sure we — I include myself — do.

I am equally sure that the modern version of faith in progress is distinctive, not only for its unbelief in divine providence, but also for its isolation. Until recent times, progress was measured against the past, so that, to quote Robert Nisbet, "the idea of reform, whether directed toward individual or social order, almost invariably carried with it the message of return, renewal, or recovery." But the rapidity of modern social evolution, which renders continuity less visible than discontinuity, and our pluralism, which dissolves history's main story-lines into so many sundry competing tales (black history, feminist history, Native American history, and so on) that the whole itself dissolves, have turned the past into a series of short newsreels, or even disconnected snapshots; and of what use is that? We cannot return to where we have not been.

Our isolation, if undesirable, is understandable. It is no surprise that our nostalgia cannot pass beyond the 1960s or 1950s. The Essenes, by contrast, wanted to go back eight hundred years to the time of David. And Pascal, when he imagined better times, actually thought about the Garden of Eden. And what of Michelangelo and Rembrandt, whose subjects as often as not belonged to pre-Christian times? Today we do not touch the past but see it dimly from afar; and its voices, among them those of heroes, fade over the distance.

In 1934 the American Historical Association, through its commission on the social sciences, said that "instruction in the social sciences should begin in the earliest years of schooling, not with the life and institutions of some people remote in time, space, and cultural development, but with the life and institutions of the surrounding community — the simple social relationships of the family and the neighborhood and the modes of providing food, clothing, shelter, medical care, education, recreation, cultural opportunities and security of person." This advice, since incorporated into the so-called expanding environments approach of our public schools, regards men and women outside immediate experience as "remote in time, space, and cultural development." The enumeration of a threefold detachment reveals an unspoken, rhetorical question. How can the past — the uncomplicated, patriarchal, undemocratic past — which is so very different from the present, be of immediate instruction? Such is the common utilitarian doubt, so lacking in imagination. Is the past not just an empty cocoon for the newly emerged present? Sidney Simon, the proponent of values clarification, has remarked that he no longer finds meaning "in the history of war or the structure of a sonnet." In other words, the past with its conventional heroes is not useful: Simon has put away childish things.

Because heroes are often adventurers, Simon's impoverishment may owe something to the fate of adventure in the Western world. Paul Zweig has shown us that whereas in the past, adventure, "the oldest, most persistent subject matter in the world," was "constitutive of culture itself, as in the Prometheus story and in other origin myths," for us —

that is, for post-Renaissance Westerners — adventure is marginal, escapist. Why? After the emergence, in late medieval times, of a merchant class independent of manor and guild, and after the philosophical doubts that inevitably trailed the Reformation, speculation and labor became "the creators of essential value." There was, on the one hand, Descartes, sitting alone and thinking himself into existence; and then, on the other hand, there was the believer in the Protestant ethic and the spirit of capitalism. Both the philosopher and the merchant regarded adventure literature as recreation at best, as illicit at worst.

Much more recently, at the end of a long process by which we have come to identify devils and muses and even God as the projected images of our invisible selves, we are all psychologists. Gilgamesh and Beowulf, however, were not analysts, nor were their chroniclers. The old tales accordingly seem naïve and unsatisfying. Zweig writes, "Our modern sense of adventure has discovered that an exploit's interior face contains its true potency"; and, in line with this, W. Jackson Bate comments, "In most novels since Thomas Mann, story and hero have been lost." Odysseus, who looks outward, not inward, is uncomplicated; and without action he ceases to be. (The year with Circe is unremarkable.) We are much more drawn to the inactive but reflective Robinson Crusoe, to the symbolic jungle of Conrad's *Heart of Darkness,* to the frustration and loneliness of Leopold Bloom in Joyce's modern *Ulysses,* and to the brooding introspection of T. E. Lawrence. The traditional heroic types, although ineradicable, now inhabit mostly popular and children's literature, where their escapist function is manifest. A well-defined beginning followed by a series of struggles from which a hero emerges happy and triumphant seems to us simplistic, mere entertainment. James Bond is comedy. Even the movies now employ the aesthetically complete scenario less than before. More and more they promote what Zweig calls "the leisure of sensibility." Our hunger in this age of existentialism is less for great accomplishments than for internal secrets; and our confusion, when it takes itself seriously, wants to read Kafka.

One might suppose that, if the old heroes are gone, and if science now rules the world, that there is honor at least for the new heroes of science. But it is not so. Scientists can no longer become heroes because their discoveries are, to Mr. and Mrs. Average, and even to Mr. and Mrs. Above-average, mostly unintelligible. Those at the frontiers of scientific knowledge belong to esoteric clubs. Their words to outsiders are pearls thrown before swine. Because only a small number could fathom his equations, Einstein himself became as much a celebrity as a hero, known more for his unkempt hair and absent-mindedness than the content of special relativity. (*TV Guide* has denied the rumor that he once guest-starred on "Gunsmoke.") Moreover, many scientific breakthroughs, like most scientific papers, are today the product of a group, not individual genius. The atom bomb came out of committee. But, notwithstanding the Spartans at the pass of Thermopylae, collectives seldom become heroes.

Perhaps the chief reason celebrities crowd the public stage is that the mass media requires daily news. The papers, the television, and the radio, in order to justify continual dissemination of their product, must ever say something new. They must never surrender to silence. Of course such mulish refusal to conform to the natural course of things cannot but be arduous. Celebrities, however, make the task possible. They can always be willingly introduced, gossiped about, and then, when attention wanes, ignored, after which still others can be hurried onto the same carousel. Their number is limitless because there is seldom anything special about them. The celebrity is, in truth, not somebody but anybody. Do they not all seem interchangeable? Like dollar bills, which can no longer be redeemed for gold or silver, each is supposed to be worth something; yet one is as good as another.

In this way the media skirts any void. It matters not that so many who thus gain our attention are asses unworthy of it. Alas, all that counts is that, like children at a parade, we are ever entranced by the media's march of images, and constantly captivated by its incessant chatter. With our minds enthralled, havoc enters our souls. We lose our poetic curiosity as well as the habit of thinking. And so we are ready for the next entertainer.

If there is indeed an instinct to emulate what appears before us, then at present we must be emulating celebrities. Observation confirms the inference. Celebrities are trendsetters. Who first models our hairstyles? Our skirt lengths? Our eyewear? Now this is not in itself objectionable. Nor do I protest that so many celebrities, stained by riotous living, are decadent, unworthy of emulation. The problem is more fundamental. It is that celebrities are not heroes — that is, they are, even when upright, too small to do us any good. Celebrities are, as their numbers necessitate, average people. This is why their sins — extramarital affairs, multiple divorces, drinking binges — are so humdrum. They are just like us. But to look at ourselves is to emulate ourselves, which means giving up "ought" for "is." To look in a mirror does not expand one's horizons. We need rather to dream, which is what heroes and poets, not celebrities, make us do.

Christopher Lasch is right: celebrities are welcome in the culture of narcissism because the narcissistic individual lacks the courage and imagination to change the self into the not-self; and whereas this is precisely the helpful demand implicitly made by traditional heroes, celebrities are not imperatives. With them there are no surprises, and we can be ourselves — a frightful notion, if one is honest. Celebrities do not encourage the humble thing, which is the reasonable thing: finding our lives by losing them. As Meister Eckhart observed, "Those who would be what they ought to be must stop being what they are."

Where is the sanity in attending to the ordinary when the imperatives upon us — "Go the extra mile," "Do not let the left hand know what the right hand is doing," "Be perfect in love, even as the heavenly Father is perfect" — are so extraordinary? The chief objection to Jesus' moral injunctions has always been that they are too difficult: the Kingdom of God is Utopia. As the Jew in Justin Martyr's *Dialogue with Trypho* remarked, the Gospel teachings are "so wonderful and so great that I suspect no one can keep them."

Leaving for another occasion defense of Jesus' ever-receding moral ideal, one thing is evident: the pious require models of old-fashioned heroic proportion, and narratives that reveal the possibilities and obligations of being "in the law of Christ." If democracy, historical criticism, the hermeneutics of suspicion, an exaggerated belief in progress, our doubts about the value of adventure, and the incessant distractions of the mass media take these things from us, then the game is up — we have lost our souls. These dragons that have captured our heroes must be either tamed or slain, so that our moral imaginations can, once again, be pressed down, shaken together, and running over.

Hebrews 11 says this: "[They] conquered kingdoms, enforced justice, received promises, stopped the mouths of lions, quenched raging fire, escaped the edge of the sword, won strength out of weakness, became mighty in war, put foreign armies to flight" (vv. 33-34). We should, against the modern habit, hold these for memories, that they might hold us. Our amnesia should not be for heroes, whose virtues are our sunlight, but for their modern usurpers, who represent the ordinary condition of humanity, which so obviously tends toward sin and sloth and mediocrity. Celebrities do not conquer kingdoms, enforce justice, receive promises, stop the mouths of lions, quench raging fires, escape the edge of the sword, win strength out of weakness, become mighty in war, put enemies to flight. Why exchange gold for pyrite?

Our lives depend upon what the wise Confucius called *Te,* the power of living virtue, that turns onlookers into itself. Here the church should — it seldom does — stand against the culture, and its members should emulate, in a new idiom, the early cenobites, who forsook the vanities and distractions of the cities for the desert, there to imitate spiritual fathers and mothers. The Christian needs to become, if I may quote the Buddha, "the unheeding sage who ignores what others toil to learn." A reverend once said that, among the smaller duties of life, few are more important than not praising where praise is not due. He was correct, except that what once was small has since grown large: the duty is now incumbent. To borrow from Paul, pay all of them their due: respect to whom respect is due, honor to whom honor is due, and inattention to whom inattention is due.

Whether Carlyle was right to assert that all religions are, in origin and essence, hero worship, Christianity at least does not refute him. Indeed, the entirety of our tradition may be summed up in a series of deathless names — Adam and Eve, Noah, Abraham and Sarah, Jacob, Joseph, Moses, David, Elijah, Isaiah, Jeremiah, John the Baptist, Mary, Jesus, and Paul, to which one may add, according to one's tradition, the saints and heroes of post-biblical times: Gregory of Nyssa and Isaac of Nineveh, or Francis of Assisi and Teresa of Avila, or Dietrich Bonhoeffer and Dorothy Day. Christianity is the interpretation of life by the light of their stories, and their deeds of faith are, as the Greeks would have put it, a law alive. Should we not then be as much preoccupied with these, our moral predecessors, the great cloud of witnesses that surrounds us, as were Aristotle and Einstein with their philosophical and scientific forebears?

T. S. Eliot argued that the literary artist must earnestly converse with history, must sense the timeless in the temporal, must conform (although not merely conform) to the living dead. How much more is all this true of the moral artist, which is what the Christian is summoned to be? Christian tradition is biography, and biography is both the guardian angel of creativity and the energy of the will.

The opposite of tradition has no name. Yet we know what it is. It is a life lived only in the present, which is necessarily an uninformed life, formed by whatever happens by. It is a life not consciously assimilated to authentic heroes, and so a life doomed to be unconsciously assimilated to bogus celebrities. It is a life not measured against the past, and so unexamined, a life not worth living.

Jesus said, "Turn the other cheek." Without his example, and without the example of the saints, the injunction has no meaning. The letter without the Spirit, which I take to mean content without context, speech without biography, present without past, kills. The Spirit, the animator of heroes, gives life.

PRAYER

CHAPTER 6

Physical Prayer

And Moses made haste to bow his head toward the earth, and worshiped.

Exodus 34:8

When people wish to pray, they arrange the body just as it suits them at that moment with a view towards moving the soul.

Augustine

I have long been emptying trays of ice. But I was thirty-seven years old before one night I was moved, for reason unknown, to study the cubes. Thereupon I noticed what I had not noticed before: that each one peaks in the middle. The discovery moved me first to thought and then to ring up an engineer for an explanation, which comes to this: an ice cube freezes and so expands from the outside in, and because five of the six walls are solid, there is finally nowhere to go but up. That explanation, however, is of no present concern — only the point that awareness does not accompany all our doings. Much of our time is spent in a sort of sleepwalking, in which we constantly fail to register countless facts about ourselves and our world. The common experience of driving down the highway and realizing that one has entirely missed the last few miles stands for our entire existence.

Our everyday somnolence does not leave us when we practice our religion. At prayer we routinely bow our heads, bend our knees, and close our eyes — all with minimal effort, and usually without wondering exactly what we are doing or why. One guesses, moreover, that, if asked, most who so act could offer no compelling account of their actions. We know not what we do.

There is no mystery in this. Often we learn only to forget; that is, much learning is the gaining of habit, the transfer of this or that to an unconscious level. Activities such as eating, walking, and reading require, once learned, no mental effort. Literature is kept near toilets because what they are for requires no attention. Much we do is automatic, second nature, what the psychologists call "preattentive." For this we should of course be grateful. Forgetfulness enables our limited processing capacities to move on to other things. We nonetheless often learn much by pondering the disregarded, among which is the subject of physical prayer.

In church and out, Christians regularly bow their heads. This might be explained, without much thought, as behavior learned through imitation. Children see their parents and others lower their heads at prayer (the cause). They naturally do likewise (the effect). Such a proposal, however, takes us nowhere. For wherever there have been people, there has been religion, and wherever there has been religion, people have bent their necks. The behavior is not confined to Christians, or to Jews and Christians, or to Moslems and Jews and Christians; it is truly universal. The Incas did this thing, as Bernabe Cobo recorded: "Facing their gods or temples and *guacas* they lowered their heads and their bodies in a profound show of humility." Surely there is some far-flung instinct that moves the religious to bow their heads. What else could explain such consistent conduct, this unconscious tradition of our species?

But people bow their heads on many occasions, not just when occupied with properly religious duties. Kings and queens have forever been honored by downcast faces. And in some cultures — one thinks especially of Asiatic manners — the bowing of one's head functions like a handshake. It is a greeting, a sign of friendship, a testimony to good as opposed to hostile intention.

Clearly the religious act of bowing the head before the transcendent has a close parallel in the secular sphere. But it would be wrong to judge either that the religious custom evolved out of secular convention or that secular ceremony borrowed from religious rite. Neither sort of bowing explains the other.

Human beings, although created in the image of God, are animals with animal instincts. There is, despite our divine dignity, nothing singular about our wanting to eat, drink, and sleep, nor anything distinctive about the forces that incite us to learn, play, and reproduce. It is not otherwise with ceremonial head-bowing.

Konrad Lorenz, the eminent modern naturalist, left a vivid record of a fight between two timber wolves, one enormous and old, the other smaller and young. The wolves began by moving in circles around each other, fangs bared. Snaps too fast for the eye eventually followed: jaw met jaw; lips started to bleed. Gradually the older wolf slowly maneuvered the younger up against a wire fence, where he stumbled in the metal netting. The old one instantly leaped upon him. But then the unexpected and incredible happened. The tumult of the two gray furies suddenly ceased even though both continued to growl angrily, the elder in a deep bass, the younger in a higher tone suggestive of fear. Standing shoulder to shoulder, pressed against each other in a stiff, strained attitude, the two animals faced the same direction. But while the muzzle of the older wolf was up against the neck of the younger, the latter turned his teeth aside and instead offered to his enemy the unprotected bend of his neck, the most vulnerable part of his body. Within an inch of the tensed muscles that covered the jugular vein, the fangs of the stronger threatened the life of the weaker. Whereas during the initial frenzy both opposed each other with their impervious teeth to the fore, at the end the defeated beast exposed its defenseless throat to a lethal bite.

Rarely does a battle between two wolves come to death, this because, when one wolf begins to dominate, the other is always able, without fleeing, to arrest the violence. This is done by suspending attack and offering the neck. With jugular exposed, field of vision restricted, and jaws turned aside and so useless, the weaker wolf surrenders; and the stronger, instead of taking advantage of a defenseless opponent, is stayed, its aggression inhibited. The encounter, after some minutes of tense stillness, with death a muscle contraction away, soon ends: the victor strides off, the loser slinks away. The act of bowing the head, of offering the neck in dire straits, is somehow programmed into a wolf's genes, as is the merciful response to it. So a superior wolf, when suddenly confronted by total vulnerability, by an offer of self-sacrifice, instantly desists and eventually lets its hapless opponent return to its lair.

The bowing instinct observed in wolves appears also in wild dogs and cats, in jackdaws and turkeys, in seagulls and herons, as well as many other animals (although apparently not in those that can effortlessly flee attacks from their own kind — doves and certain deer, for instance). In the judgment of biologists, the widespread behavior arose in the course of evolution, to counter the development of dangerous weapons in beasts of prey. Lorenz suggests that "should a dog or wolf unrestrainedly and unaccountably bite the neck of his pack-mates and actively execute the movement of shaking them to death, then his species . . . would certainly be exterminated within a short span of time." This seems the right guess.

But the observation for us is that human beings also exhibit the prevalent instinct. This is why, in the annals of military history, the hero who has lost will often, instead of retreating, throw aside shield, helmet, and sword and fall prostrate before the champion. It is also why, in Joshua 10:24, humbled kings offer their vulnerable necks to the feet of victorious Israelites: "Come near, put your feet upon the necks of these kings." Josephus similarly tells us that, when the Jews in Jerusalem protested Pontius Pilate putting Roman military standards in the temple, their response to being surrounded by the governor's soldiers was this: "Casting themselves prostrate and baring their throats, they declared that they gladly welcomed death rather than . . . transgress the laws." Surely the old practice, now little observed, of doffing one's hat in the presence of another, and so exposing the head, is, as Lorenz guessed, a vestige of the old instinct. So too the ceremony that traditionally opens a sumo match. Before engagement a wrestler and his opponent face each other, bend waists (as best they can), and then bow heads. This show of respect, this prefatory calm, is always mutual, and we cannot imagine one giant striking at the other when heads are supposed to be down.

Tragically, the rules of sumo do not always hold outside the game. With the relatives of Cain, who are not so honorable as wolves, one never knows the upshot of human pleas for mercy. Will waving a white flag in battle lead to imprisonment or herald death? We read in Homer,

> Then Tors, Alastor's son, sank at his knees
> and begged the Akhaian to take him prisoner,
> to spare a man his own age, not to kill
> but pity him. How witless, to imagine
> Achilles could be swayed! No moderate temper,
> no mild heart was in this man, but harsh
> and deadly purpose. Tors embraced his knees,
> beseeching him, but with his blade he opened
> a wound below the liver.

There was good reason why Jesus, when he commanded his followers to turn the other cheek, made no promises about the outcome, and good reason why his beatitudes end with future tenses: "will be comforted," "will be satisfied," "will obtain mercy." The meek have not yet inherited the earth: that is eschatology. In this unjust world, submission as often as not means death: the lamb is led to the slaughter, the Jew to the oven. Passivity invites extinction.

We can, backtracking now to the main subject, understand why people bow their heads in prayer. It is because, before the divine, they know themselves to be defeated animals. Despite the story of Jacob at Bethel, there is no wrestling with God, if by that is meant a real contest of power. "What are human beings that you are mindful of them, mortals that you care for them?" (Ps. 8:4, NRSV). Omnipotence has no opposition. The human beast can accordingly do nothing but surrender, that is, incline neck and ask for clemency — and then hope that God will respond not as Achilles but as the wolf, with compassion.

Lines from the Eastern Orthodox Vespers come to mind. At one point the priest calls out, "Let us bow our heads unto the Lord." He follows with this: "O Lord our God, who didst bow the heavens and come down for the salvation of mankind, look upon thy servants and thine inheritance; for unto thee, the awful judge, who yet lovest mankind, have thy servants bowed their heads and submissively inclined their necks, awaiting not succor from men but entreating thy mercy. . . ." Here the bowing of the head is interpreted as an act of submission — "submissively inclined their necks" — which is simultaneously a prayer for mercy from the awful judge — "entreating thy mercy." All this accords with my contention. Bowing the head, according to the Vespers text, expresses vulnerability and helplessness. It is physical eloquence, a corporeal plea that the stronger will show kindness to the weaker.

If all this is so, we know not only why religious people bow their heads but also why they often kneel. The two acts go together. When one turkey offers its neck to another, it also collapses its legs. This is likewise true of other animals. For legs are weapons as well as the means for flight. To collapse them is to render them useless, so that there can be neither attack nor retreat. Kneeling is part of the ritual of surrender; it is aggression giving up on itself and gambling with pacifism.

It is the same with human beings. Our intuitive reaction to encountering the holy is to adopt the posture of a beaten animal (which is, incidentally, also the posture of the guillotine victim, another parallel I like to think about). This is why the Buddhists kneel at shrines, and why the old Romans knelt at sacred temples. With Divinity there can be no contest and no absconding: "Thou canst do all things" and "Whither shall I flee from Thy Spirit?" The Most High can only be met with pleas for mercy. To be instead "stiff-necked" — a most appropriate biblical term for intractable pride — is folly. This is why we instinctively do just the opposite and bend the knees. As it says in the Psalms, "O come, let us worship and bow down, let us kneel before the LORD, our Maker!" (95:6). And as Origen wrote, when discussing deportment in prayer, "As for bending one's knees, this is required when one is going to confess sins before God and beseech Him for the healing of forgiveness. One ought to know that this is the attitude proper to those who humble and submit themselves, as Paul says: 'For this cause I bend my knees to the Father of whom all paternity on heaven and earth is named.'"

That bending the knees and bowing the head are evidences of the same impulse appears from this, that it usually feels awkward to buckle the legs without bending the neck: the former naturally pulls down the latter. One remembers how Elijah prayed for rain: "He bowed himself down upon the earth, and put his face between his knees" (1 Kings 18:42).

Having suggested that people typically bow their heads and bend their knees during prayer because they are heeding an old surrender instinct, I should like similarly to explain yet a third practice commonly done in prayer. I refer to the folding together of hands, so frequently the physical correlate of verbal begging.

Hand-folding, like knee-bending and head-bowing, has been widely practiced: it is as traditional in Nepali Buddhism as in Italian Catholicism. It appears in ancient religious texts, in old Hindu sculpture (the so-called *anjali mudra*), on Byzantine icons, in Renaissance paintings, and in contemporary American churches, both Catholic and Protestant. Once more we are looking at something so prevalent that it invites a biological exegesis.

Hands are, for human beings, the primary weapons. They strike out at others and are likewise the instruments we use to hurl or aim offensive projectiles — rocks, arrows, bullets. How did Goliath fall? "David put his hand in his bag and took out a stone, and slung it, and struck the Philistine on his forehead" (1 Sam. 17:49). It is only to be expected that people, who instinctively adopt a posture of passivity and submission before God, fold their hands together for prayer. Such folding is a reflex action of yielding and nonresistance, a disarming of ourselves. One cannot use the hands for violence while they are uselessly holding each other. By this gesture, then, those at prayer physically display the spiritual truth that regarding ultimate matters human hands can do nothing.

In the Bible and early Christian tradition, however, it is more characteristic that prayer is made not with hands joined but with hands spread forth:

"Hear the voice of my supplication, as I cry to thee for help, as I lift up my hands toward thy most holy sanctuary." (Ps. 28:2)

"Let my prayer be counted as incense before thee, and the lifting up of my hands as an evening sacrifice!" (Ps. 141:2)

"I desire then that in every place the men should pray, lifting holy hands without anger or quarreling." (1 Tim. 2:8)

The Sumerians, Egyptians, and Etruscans spread their arms for prayer; and in Homer there is this: "At the ships they tried to stand and fight, and shouted to each other, calling out with hands held high to all the gods as well." In old Roman and early Christian art, moreover, a human figure with two arms raised symmetrically, palms facing forward — the so-called orant — is the standard representation of piety.

But the chief observation is that the gesture is not confined to religious activities. We have all seen it in other contexts, if only in films and on television. Worshipers with raised hands are just like soldiers surrendering and criminals cornered by the police ("Hands up! You're under arrest."). Raising the hands with palms open reveals the absence of a weapon and leaves the vulnerable torso unprotected. It also renders the arm temporarily impotent, for, as the boxer illustrates, only a drawn or cocked arm can deliver force. Undoubtedly hands are raised in public ritual and private devotion because the individual's relationship to the holy, felt intuitively, is that of captive to captor.

There is a theological lesson in the involvement of the body in prayer. It is this: even in the most other-worldly activity, the worshiper remains an earthbound animal. Prayer is not a leaving behind of the body. It is instead an act of the entire individual. Even if prayer "raises one from earth to heaven" (Gregory Palamas), even if it gives detachment "from anything subject to flux and change" and induces "rest in motionless spiritual repose" (Gregory of Nyssa), all this cannot mean a splitting in two of the self. Only death does that. No, in prayer the whole person is offered to God. This is why, in Origen's words, "even at the very highest climax of contemplation we do not for a moment forget the Incarnation," that is, God's involvement with human flesh.

Paul exhorted the readers of his letter to the Romans, "By the mercies of God, . . . present your *somata* as a living sacrifice, holy and well-pleasing to God" (12:1). The word left untranslated, *somata,* means, as Calvin put it, "the totality of which we are composed." When prayer is rightly made, matter is joined to spirit, and together the two seek the divine grace. Perhaps in this way we fulfill the Pauline imperative: "Glorify God in your body."

So far I have considered certain activities that display our kinship with other creatures. There is, however, something else often done in prayer that isolates us from the rest of the animal kingdom. I refer to the common closing of the eyes. It is true that this is another element of the surrender response, for blindness greatly adds to vulnerability. But it is also true that shutting the eyes in prayer eliminates visual stimulation and so helps the mind to shift its attention, helps it to move from the sensual plane to an inner cell. We close the outer eyes not only because of the surrender response but also because we seek something that can be seen only with the inner eyes. This entry into blackness, wherein our religious imagination thrives, is not the activity of wolves.

Whether it be petition, intercession, adoration, or contemplation, prayer is attention — that is, focused awareness, directed consciousness. It is a state in which one strives to dampen awareness of the outer world and to replace it with an acute awareness of the inner world. The presupposition is that full attention can fall upon only one world at a time — for the same reason that two conversations cannot be followed at once. As Aldous Huxley once remarked, "Thy kingdom come" entails "our kingdom go."

But this is work, for attention rapidly flits from this to that, ever hovering, never alighting. Like Noah's dove, it does not land. Attention, moreover, wanes before the familiar, and the unlighted, inner chamber of prayer is familiar; we know it all too well. Day after day it offers to the mind's eye nothing more than the same empty darkness. Those at prayer are like a Jewish high priest of the Second Temple Period who, on the Day of Atonement, entered an arkless Holy of Holies to observe that the most sacred precinct, the intersection of heaven and earth, contained absolutely nothing except black walls, as though God were a great blank. I remember how I prayed when I was ten years old: my mind entered a little room with an empty throne. No one was there.

As if the boredom bred of familiarity with our inner selves were not enough deterrent to prolonged or profound prayer, God is said to be never-changing, the same yesterday, today, and forever. But experience teaches that novelty is the magnet of attention, and that attention lets go of sameness. This is why background music fades in and out of awareness, and why the ticking of a clock eventually recedes from consciousness. Awareness feeds upon fluctuation. The fact can even be measured:

monotonous stimuli produce a progressive decline in the voltage of evoked brain potentials. But God and God's love are, from one point of view, monotonous stimuli, for they are always present and never-changing. They are therefore not likely of themselves to arouse increased clarity of consciousness. Closing the eyes in search of God can make us yawn.

Even if one has no prejudice against preternatural visions and voices, such things must be reckoned relatively rare. Most lives of prayer pass without the appearance of shining angels or the guidance of Socratic daemons. While many do cultivate vague feelings of a transcendent presence, customarily the Deity's communication is at best subliminal, nothing more than an indistinct prod for our informed imaginations. God remains veiled in darkness and so is apt to lose our attention. I sometimes think the Divinity is like a child who does not know that the game of hide-and-seek is done.

One can tell when a dog comes to increased attention. Its ears prick up, its muscles tense, and its eyes look forward. And so it is with us. Attention upon a fact in the terrene world has physiological correlates: the pupils dilate, the heart rate goes up, the ears become more discerning. But precisely what gains attention varies from individual to individual. Such variation, we now know, derives in part from the genes. Temperaments are inbred.

Yet we also know that both the quality of attention and its ability to tarry are much affected by past experience. Awareness can, for example, be befogged by chronic anxiety, just as it can be clarified by certain exercises prescribed by Theravadan Buddhism. The circumstance matters for the practice of prayer.

The eye is our most important sensory organ because it brings us so much information — more than the nose, the tongue, the hand, or even the ear. In Descartes's words, "sight is the most comprehensive" sense. We do not smell before we cross the road. Anthropologists speculate that our arboreal ancestors, unlike terrestrial beasts, needed seeing more than hearing or smelling, and evolution cooperated. That is why there are so many more nerve endings in the optic nerve than in the auditory nerve or olfatory nerve. In any case, as Augustine observed, although only the eyes see, we sometimes say "See how loud it is," or "See how it smells," or "See how it tastes," or "See how hard it is." We do not, on the other hand, say "Hear how it glows," or "Smell how bright it is," or "Taste how it shines," or "Feel how it glitters." Again, when we understand, we say "I see," not "I hear" or "I smell." Obviously our attentive abilities are very much a function of visual experience. Beginning in infancy, when our eyes struggle to focus, our minds are molded by what we see.

One may illustrate by referring to the purported effect of so-called educational television upon children. Although the findings have been disputed, more than one study has concluded that pre-schoolers regularly exposed to *Sesame Street* tend to have shorter attention spans than others not so exposed. Assuming this result to be true, its interpretation is evident. Those accustomed to the delight of rapidly moving images and bright colors — the dancing yellow Big Bird, for example — are more prone to tedium before a real-life teacher in a less vivid setting. Excitation enlarges the appetite for more excitation, and there is a natural anesthesia in anything less.

One understands the traditional wisdom, no longer in favor, of placing children in sparsely decorated cubicles. It is only time that teaches us not to notice things, only age that bestows discrimination between the important and the unimportant. So one should not want young learners surrounded by potential distractions. Protracted attention is the soul of learning, and authentic education eventually requires concentration upon facts unadorned by exciting stimuli. One might urge that the more children accustom themselves to the unexciting, the better learners they will be. And yet the contemporary tendency is to put audiovisual materials into textbooks and into curricula, to fill them with pictures, maps, diagrams, and illustrations.

The advent of educational television is just one facet of the modern multiplication and consumption of images. Only in the last century and a quarter have images become, to quote Jacques Ellul, "a collective force" modifying "the psychic structures of a group." The first newspaper photograph appeared in 1880. Think about a life lived out before the Civil War. How many human faces did it behold? And how many pictures, how many photographs and paintings, book illustrations and billboards did it see? While such things cannot be counted, the number must be merely a fraction of what it is for a life lived now, a fact so memorably interpreted in Daniel Boorstin's *The Image*. Our visual inflation has far outrun our economic inflation. In our contemporary world even dictionaries have pictures; and who among us, upon taking up, let's say, a new biography, fails to glance at the photographs first?

With the insertion of images into books, magazines, and newsprint, and then the triumphal entry of movies and television, the varied faces of nature have progressively receded from view; and a myriad of manufactured images, almost all of them short-lived, many of them literally "motion pictures," have displaced them. Whereas staring used to mean, by definition, looking fixedly upon one person or thing, now, in the age of movies and TV, it can mean prolonged gazing upon a series of things — like looking out the train window. But what does this new sort of gazing, especially our collective dreaming before screens, do to us?

Our eyes now give us what we get from caffeine: a heightened alertness but also an increase in distractibility. The more images there are, the less time, by necessity, we have to penetrate each. One would expect attention spans, which are not immutable, to retrogress. Even if certain social scientists and educational theorists, who little investigate this particular proposition, still want to reserve judgment, Chestertonian common sense and the anecdotal evidence suffice to persuade. The overwhelming quantity of fleeting yet hypnotic images has reduced the quality of awareness. As Marshall McLuhan prophesied, the objects of perception have altered the perceiving subjects; what we have made has remade us. Everybody has Attention Deficit Disorder.

The evolution of the TV advertisement offers compelling illustration. The commercials of the 1950s unfolded at a leisurely pace. Their pleasant images showed themselves to us for several seconds. But an acceleration began in the 1960s and has continued since: images have progressively occupied less and less time. At present there are commercials that feature three or four disparate scenes a second. Among my acquaintances, those over forty rarely comprehend or enjoy the swift sequences; and surely such speed would not have been seductive in the 1950s.

But it is certain that the advertisers know what they are doing. They have discovered that today's consumer disposition more and more welcomes the ever-increasing cascade of images, that it delights in the arousal of attention but not in sustained focus upon one thing. Our eyes are ever hungry. For most of us, the slow unwinding of a novel's complex story line is less enchanting than the disjointed routine of the stand-up comic, whose parade of isolated one-liners is the verbal correlate of the disconnected pictures of the soft-drink commercial. So our entertainment brings transient titillation, which means vision without comprehension. We behold form without attending to substance. Seeing, we do not see.

But the forms often have little substance anyway. Our voracious eyes now recurrently feed upon a common bread that lacks a real presence. The pictures are so many that they can rarely be little more than superficial symbols, brief emotional tugs. Rapidity means there is so much more to see, and nothing much worth seeing. Our world is again baroque: the surplus of images, the optic cacophony, overwhelms reason and sires a phantasmagoric confusion. Were Leonardo da Vinci alive today, perhaps he would no longer assert that to see is to know. It is no wonder that in so many modern pieces of art the eyes are without spark or even mutilated, or altogether absent: it is revenge for the lies of the modern spectacle.

Should we not wonder how the changing content of our visual experience affects our religious experience? Might not habits and expectations and pleasures carried to us by the contemporary flood of images disincline one to pass much waking time with eyes closed? I am sure, although I can offer no proof, that those who spend hours every day in front of a TV pray less than they otherwise might, not because they have less faith, nor because their morals have been corrupted, nor because their time is consumed by the tube. Rather, their attention spans, like their imaginations, have been made lazy. If prayer is sustained concentration upon the seemingly unexciting, how well can it be practiced by those habituated more and more to just the opposite? Surely the great sin of the modern world is indolence. It is so easy to lie back in a recliner and let the snowstorm of pictures fall upon the mind's black ground.

Perhaps we can live with the guilt of our prayerlessness because there is now a compensatory misery in prayer, a misery begotten by our attenuated attention spans and our loathing of sensory vacancy. In an age that procreates too many images, it surely requires a confident athlete to enter a mental darkness where the words and pictures (if there be any at all) are endogenous, a darkness in which attention must struggle to focus upon things not sensually alluring. Our inflated ocular appetite gives us hunger pains when it enters the darkness of prayer. This is not to imply that we should share the iconoclasm of eighth- and ninth-century Byzantium or the Protestant Reformers' hostility to visual representation. Sight is good, and surely we should pray with Augustine, "Thanks be to you, O Lord, for all that we see." But should we not also wonder what the scriptural warning about "the lust of the eyes" has to say to us? Surely we can find our own meaning in the Bantu proverb "The eye is the source of the lie."

Aldous Huxley said, "If recollection, or the overcoming of distractions, has never been more necessary than now . . . it has also, one may guess, never been so difficult." We too often stare at artificial sources of arousal, and their animated lights easily seduce us. But the closing of the eyes for prayer, an innate act of wisdom, shows us that often we rather need the darkness. The shutting out of light is a sacred instinct that should move us to deny ourselves and to undo what we have turned ourselves into. Perhaps we should figuratively emulate the wise Democritus, who allegedly blinded himself in order to see with his mind. Certainly we can remember Samson, who regained his strength after losing his eyes. The divine dusk beckons. We must unlearn our boredom.

CHAPTER 7

Hitting a Home Run

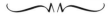

And Jesus answered them, "Have faith in God. Truly, I say to you, whoever says to this mountain, 'Be taken up and cast into the sea,' and does not doubt in his heart, but believes that what he says will come to pass, it will be done for him. Therefore I tell you, whatever you ask in prayer, believe that you have received it, and it will be yours."

Mark 11:22-24

And to keep me from being too elated by the abundance of revelations, a thorn was given me in the flesh, a messenger of Satan, to harass me, to keep me from being too elated. Three times I besought the Lord about this, that it should leave me; but he said to me, "My grace is suffiecient for you, for my power is made perfect in weakness."

2 Corinthians 12:7-9

The year was 1967, and I was eleven years old. The week-night dinner was finished, and I, without any homework, was relaxing in the bathtub, listening to St. Louis Cardinals' baseball. The game was close and in the latter innings. The announcer, Harry Caray — he had not gone to Chicago yet — was tense. So was I. Who was at the plate — Curt Flood, Orlando Cepeda, Joe Torre — I do not recall. Nor do I remember the score, nor how many runners were on base. But I can tell you exactly what I thought, or rather what strange idea entered my mind, as the count went to full, three balls and two strikes: If only I don't move a muscle, if only I lie perfectly still in this nice warm water, the batter will, with the very next pitch, hit a home run. Of course the reason I remember all this is that, as it happened, the batter drove the ball out of the park.

My experience in the bath stands for a class of experiences. For, to judge from conversations with others, something peculiar commonly happens to spectators caught up in a sporting event. From somewhere within will come, unbidden, the thought that one can, by behaving in a certain way, influence the outcome from afar.

The curious notion takes many forms. It may, for instance, occur to a man while he sits on his couch watching Monday-night football that, if only he finishes his chips and dip before the current series of commercials is over, his team's next drive will end with a touchdown. Or perhaps he may imagine that if he uses the bathroom before the two-minute warning, his team will hold on and win. The broadcasters themselves regularly indulge in analogous behavior. Those who listen much to basketball on the radio or watch it much on TV have often heard an announcer confidently declare that Player X is quite a fine free-throw shooter and then, when X goes on to miss the next free throw, confide — half seriously — that it was bad luck to acclaim X's ability: "Looks like I shouldn't have said anything." Behind such confiding lies the fantastic feeling that some causal correlation can obtain between a spectator's words and a player's performance; and the inkling, however unreasonable, is forceful enough to materialize as a very public utterance.

Although the conscious mind knows that our distant hopes and cheers do not determine the outcomes of sporting events, some part of us refuses reason. It appears that we are, as a species, strongly inclined to act as though we have extraordinary abilities. Some primeval part of us is never fully persuaded that we influence the world only through direct physical contact with other things. There seems rather to be an unconscious inclination to imagine that directed thought can act at a distance, that we can move more than our bodies and the things they touch. We are infected with magical thinking.

With this in mind, I should now like to return to the Scriptures, to Jesus' word to us that we can move mountains with prayer. Do we not have to begin by candidly asking about the relationship between Jesus' incredible promise and magical thinking? What was he doing when he assured people that whatever they ask in prayer, they will receive, if only they believe? Can anything be more obviously opposed to all reason and experience?

The questions are the more pressing because Jesus himself, Mark tells us, asked in Gethsemane for the cup to pass from him — "Abba, Father, all things are possible to thee; remove this cup from me" (Mark 14:36) — and the cup did not pass from him. He got crucified. How do we understand this? Does Jesus' own experience falsify his pledge? Does the text here deconstruct itself?

I suppose one might retort, "Come on, quit being impious. Jesus didn't really mean it; he didn't really want to escape arrest and crucifixion, which he talked about so much beforehand. That's why he qualified his request with 'yet not what I want, but what you want.'" Well, maybe. Yet it still seems to me that if "Remove this cup from me" was not heartfelt and sincere, then no prayer ever was. I at least think that Jesus meant what he said at the time that he said it, and he had faith overflowing. So why, I must ask myself, if his promise to us about prayer is not bogus, did he not get what he asked for?

If this example does not suffice, there is Paul: "Three times I appealed to the Lord about this, that it would leave me, but he said to me, 'My grace is sufficient for you, for power is made perfect in weakness'" (2 Cor. 12:8-9). Why did not Paul get what he asked for? Is it because he did not have enough faith? Or did his prayer, like that of Jesus, stand under the proviso "Thy will be done"? Perhaps it did. But that just hands us another puzzle. What is the point of telling us we get what we want if, in the end, we really only get what God wants?

There are, of course, clever theological answers to these simple questions, and maybe some of those answers make good sense. Moreover, it is my guess, for what it is worth, that Jesus' saying about moving mountains is an instance of Semitic hyperbole, the sort of thing one finds all the time in the rabbis, in the same class with a camel going through the eye of a needle. It is a poetic and memorable way of exhorting people to pray more and with more confidence.

In this instance, however, uncovering the proper interpretation of our text is perhaps less edifying than unmasking its misinterpretation and misuse. For the saying about moving mountains becomes dangerous when, as happens all the time, our magical minds get hold of it, when we forget Gethsemane and forget Paul's thorn in the flesh and thus unwittingly endorse those anthropologists who contend that religion is just magic in a new phase. Our ever-present temptation is to turn God into Santa Claus, to try to influence the Divinity the way we seek to influence a baseball game from the living room. If we are nice, not naughty, if we say our prayers just right, surely we will get the goods.

I recently saw a sign in front of a church: "No Prayer Is No Power!" The next week the same sign said, "Prayer Is Power." But the Gospel is not, as might be implied by these potentially misleading slogans, some new, secret way of getting the things we might otherwise happen to hanker after. And this, after all, is a very good thing. For human nature is fallen, and much is hidden from our minuscule minds, and I for one think God would be pretty stupid to let us have what we want. In J. R. R. Tolkien's *Lord of the Rings*, the glorious elf queen Galadriel refuses to accept from Frodo the Hobbit the great ring of power. For she knows that even though she could conquer the Dark Lord with it, in the end even she, as good as she is, would become evil with the exercise of more power than she already has. She is wise. We too are wise if we know not only, as the proverb has it, that power corrupts but further that the will to power corrupts our prayers.

I speak from miserable experience. My late father, canonized in my mind, followed his eclectic new-age theology rather than his son's exegesis and sadly took Jesus' promise of omnipotent prayer literally. He believed that, if only he had faith, real faith, his business woes would, as if by magic, disappear, and that his wife would, as if by magic, treat him kindly once again. But his wife broke his heart, and his business went bankrupt, and he died a disillusioned old man, thinking either that he had not had enough faith or that his religion had been all wrong. One of the last sentences from his cancer-filled head was the question, "Son, what does it all mean?" This, from the world's greatest optimist, wrenched my heart and haunts me still.

Surely he had faith. It was his religion, his theology, that was all wrong. It is not that he should not have prayed. And it is not that he shouldn't have hoped. It is rather that he should not have believed in magic. He was like me in the bathtub, supposing that things beyond his control would come under his control if he could just get the right religious feeling. He should have known better. He should have known that his faith had become warped by a fantasy, by a self-centered, baseless coping mechanism. He should have known from honest experience that there is no consistent correlation between what the saints pray for and what the saints get, which is why we walk by faith, not by sight. Isaiah said, "Truly you are a God who hides yourself." If all our prayers were answered, this would not be true, would it?

My father should also have known that if just the first twenty years of his life witnessed the starving of the Ukraine, the carnage of World War II, and the gassing of the chosen people, then maybe the Supreme Being who did not stop those things might not, no matter how strong my father's faith, keep his everyday life in Wichita, Kansas, free from misfortune and misery. God saw the creation and called it good, but leukemia eats little children. This is a fact, and no amount of praying will ever undo it. We cannot pray away the sins of the world. We still say "Thy kingdom come" because it has not yet come. This remains the brutal world that crucified Jesus. The Ukrainians prayed and the soldiers prayed and the Jews prayed — and the ends of so many were beyond cruel. At this moment the anguished parents of cancer-gnawed little boys and girls all over the world pray and pray and pray, begging for a miracle, and many — thank God not all, but many — will see nothing except protracted agony. It is not because they do not have enough faith. God forbid that we ever entertain such a stupid and pitiless thought, or that we naïvely suppose that while terrible things may happen to our neighbor, of course God will make sure that we, if only we say our prayers and have enough faith, are spared. What arrogant, irrational, profane nonsense.

However we wish to interpret God's apparent response to our prayers, when we pray, we are not magicians. God will be what God will be; the Creator is beyond our manipulation. God is absolutely free, free to give us exactly what we ask for — perhaps sometimes we see this — but just as free to respond in unfathomable ways, even in ways that appear to take no notice of us and make the atheist next door look smart; I know I've seen this. Sometimes indeed we are reduced to the confession of Job: I will trust in God though God slay me.

So the point is this. We must separate our spiritual lives from our magical instincts. We should heed Jesus and say our prayers, and we should trust in our good God to give us good gifts; and we should sincerely bless God when things seem to be going well. But we must equally not be naïve and fool ourselves into imagining that we can, so to speak, hit home runs from the bathtub, or that we have some sort of magical power that, thank God, we really do not have and really should not want.

CHAPTER 8

From Statistics to Silence

If someone prays he either deserves to get what he prays for or he does not. If he does deserve it, then he will get it even if he does not pray for it. But if he does not deserve it, he will not get it even if he does pray for it. . . . For it is not the case that someone who does deserve it but fails to pray for it no longer deserves it for the simple reason that he has not prayed for it. Neither is it so that the one who does not deserve to get it but did pray for it does not deserve it for the simple reason that he has prayed for it. On the contrary, the one who deserves to get it without bothering the gods deserves it even more.

Maximus of Tyre

It ["Thy will be done"] means that your will and God's will may not be the same. It means there's a good possibility that you won't get what you pray for. It means that in spite of your prayers, you are going to suffer. It means you may be crucified.

Wendell Berry

Prayer means that we penetrate through the outward appearances of things to the truth and to the real meaning of our life which springs from God.

Wilhelm Bousset

Prayer is the work of the heart, not of the lips.

Defensor Grammaticus

I sometimes ask myself, Why should I ask God for anything? Why petition omniscience? Does not the heavenly Father, as Jesus assured us, already know what we need before we ask? As it says in the Psalms, "Even before a word is on my tongue, lo, O LORD, thou knowest it altogether" (139:4). Immanuel Kant asserted that a request made of God is "a superstitious illusion," for "it is no more than a stated wish directed to a Being who needs no such information regarding the inner disposition of the wisher; therefore nothing is accomplished by it, and it discharges none of the duties to which, as commands of God, we are obligated."

I also wonder from time to time why we should pray to one who, because full of beneficence, should require no prompting to make things as good on earth as they are in heaven. As Edgar Sheffield Brightman commented, "if there is a good God, it is absurd to ask him to be better." Origen long ago expressed the natural sentiment when he wrote these words: "It is fitting that he, being father and maker of all, who loves all the things that are, and abhors nothing which he has made, should order in safety all that has to do with each one, even without prayer, like a father provides for his little children, and does not wait for them to ask."

Again, how can we expectantly ask God for something if, as the Christian tradition informs us, every request stands under the modifying clause "Thy will be done"? Friedrich Schleiermacher urged that petition for anything more than just "God's will" — a rather vague generality — is "a lapse into magic." Socrates may already have thought something similar. Xenophon in any case tells us that the sage prayed simply, "Give me that which is best for me," for Socrates believed that not he but the gods know best what the good things are. C. S. Lewis, although he did not reach Schleiermacher's skeptical conclusion, nonetheless confessed inability to reconcile the counsel to pray "Thy will be done" with his Lord's seemingly improbable assurance that "whatever you ask in prayer, you will receive, if you have faith" (Matt. 21:22).

There is yet another problem. Do we believe that God's mind can change? Omniscience and the doctrine of divine immutability seem to exclude the possibility. God is the same yesterday, today, and forever. Yet if, unlike Apollo and Athena, God's purposes never swerve, how can our prayers induce the Divinity to do this rather than that? Can we really imagine that God, like the unjust judge, can be worn out by importunity? Aquinas was familiar with the difficulty: "Prayer is a way in which we bring someone round to our own view, so that he will do what we ask him to do. But God's mind is unchanging and immovable. . . . So again it seems inappropriate to pray to God."

Samuel Johnson, as Boswell tells us, remarked, "To reason philosophically on the nature of prayer . . . [is] very unprofitable." One understands the sentiment. Thinking about petitionary prayer can lead — and in the cases of Kant and Schleiermacher did lead — to prayer's cessation, or at least to not asking for anything much in particular.

Of course, such thinking need not do so. Religious people are quite accustomed to doing and believing all sorts of things that pass understanding. Moreover, and in partial refutation of Johnson's remark, the sophisticated theological literature on prayer, beginning with Origen's delightful treatise *On Prayer*, does not just stump the intellect: it also sometimes edifies.

In this chapter, however, it is my initial aim not to edify but rather more modestly to sink to the depths of mundane cynicism and ask, Does anyone have a good reason for supposing that God answers prayer?

A little over a hundred years ago, Sir Francis Galton noted that "the question regards a matter of fact . . . that appears to be a very suitable topic for statistical enquiry." Galton himself took up the task. Starting from the plausible premise that ministers and priests pray more often than do lawyers, he surmised that the former should, on account of their many petitions, live longer. So he compared the average life expectancies of the two groups. The results were disillusioning. As unjust as it may seem, lawyers, he found, live as long as priests and ministers. Galton concluded that "the inexorable requirements of solid fact" undo "belief in the efficacy of prayer."

Despite Galton's unhappy conclusion, hordes of people remain confident that God hears and answers their prayers. The chief reason, perhaps, is that they have witnessed occasions on which a request to God was made, after which its realization followed. That, for many, is enough.

It should not be enough. Although we may all freely grant that fulfillment sometimes follows request, that scarcely settles the matter of cause and effect. That two things are linked in our minds does not require their causal connection in the world. When Navajos danced for rain and it thereafter poured, they credited their dance. We, unbelievers in the Navajo religion, rather credit coincidence. I remember B. F. Skinner's hungry pigeons. They received food at regular intervals without any reference to their behavior. If, however, food first came while a bird was, say, turning clockwise, it would thereafter turn clockwise more often; and when another pellet would come while it was thus turning, the behavior would be reinforced all the more and so engaged in even more often. Skinner argued that his pigeons were superstitious, that they all too easily formed bogus conceptions of cause and effect.

Are we, in the matter of prayer, any different than Skinner's birds? Of those now suffering financial distress, many undoubtedly will, in the normal course of events, soon see better days. Further, among those to whom improved fortune comes, many, we can be assured, will have prayed for such improvement. So might they not credit God for their prosperity? Even if God never does anything at all, there will still be people praying for more money as well as people getting more money as well as people belonging to both groups. That is, there will still be people who both pray and obtain.

The same sort of observation also shows us that we can easily doubt claims to have been healed by prayer. Although many people are now gravely ill, not all of them will die. A good number will, with or without medical assistance, and with or without divine intervention, survive to see better days. And of that number, surely a significant percentage will have prayed for health. So even if it is only through the blessings of a godless happenstance, there will always be some who get well after saying their prayers.

The point is even sharper because (1) we cannot tell a very good religious story about those whose fervent and faithful prayers escort them only to pain and death, and (2) our modern medical science — in this it has finally caught up with the ancient Greek physicians — recognizes the effectiveness of pharmacologically inert substances, that is, placebos. Doctors have effectively eliminated angina, retarded cancer, reversed arthritis, eradicated warts, erased migraines, and beat multiple sclerosis by prescribing milk-sugar pills. (Bad-tasting medicines usually work even better.) Somehow — this is the same "somehow" that hypnosis confronts us with — the mind can, when tricked into the right state, work wonders. This may be why antibiotics, which are ineffective against viruses, nonetheless often rapidly rid patients of virally induced sore throats. Sir William Osler, the famous Edwardian physician, had the placebo in mind when he said, "We should use new remedies quickly while they are still efficacious."

The productive placebo is the fruit of faith: belief in the efficacy of something can make it so. Patients, through faith, become the physicians who heal themselves. This makes one think more than twice about healings attributed to prayer, especially as religious texts worldwide ascribe to faith restorative powers. If in Mark 5 a woman is congratulated because her faith has saved her, in Philostratus's *Life of Apollonius* a man is counseled that he yet suffers because the healing god Asclepius gives health only "to those who desire it." It is the same in Taoism and Shinto: there too faith is the handmaiden of healing. This is just what knowledge of placebos should lead us to expect.

Should this be the skeptical end of the matter? Dr. Randy Byrd, a cardiologist and onetime associate professor of medicine at the University of California, some time ago claimed to demonstrate that prayer works even without the patient's psychosomatic self-help.

In a double-blind, randomized study conducted in the coronary care unit at San Francisco General Hospital, Byrd divided 393 patients — all of them unaware of the experiment — into two groups. One hundred ninety-two patients were prayed for by five to seven individuals (of Protestant, Catholic, and Jewish faith). The remaining 201 patients were left unassigned.

The results, published in the *Medical Tribune,* appear suggestive. The patients who were prayed for suffered fewer complications in three areas:

- Only six suffered pulmonary edema (water on the lungs), whereas eighteen in the other group were so stricken.

- Only three required antibiotics, as opposed to sixteen of those bereft of prayer.
- Not one received intubation; but twelve in the control group required such.

To have much meaning, however, these results obviously require replication. Some have made the attempt. In 1969, Dr. Platon J. Collip, chairman of the pediatrics department of Meadowbrook Hospital, New York, selected eighteen children with leukemia who were receiving similar treatment. Ten families were told to pray for ten of the children; the other eight were left as the control group. As reported in the *Medical Times,* eight of the ten were, after six months, still alive, whereas six of the eight were dead. But does this really show us anything?

While their reports seem at first provocative, neither Dr. Collip nor Dr. Byrd can have thought through what he was doing. The sick usually pray for themselves and have others praying for them; and, for obvious reason, neither Dr. Byrd nor Dr. Collip could insure it was otherwise with their so-called control groups. It is indeed against all probability that either supposed control group was devoid of individuals for whom families and churches offered repeated petitions. Mitchell Krucoff, a professor at Duke University Medical School and a participant in even more recent attempts to study the therapeutic effects of prayer, has admitted, "The question of whether prayer works cannot be addressed scientifically. As prayer is going on all the time, there is no true control group to study."

A truly convincing study would require that a control group consist entirely of lonely atheists and/or orphaned infants — that is, of people who neither pray for themselves nor have others praying for them. (Alternatively, why not just examine the check-in and check-out records of hospitals to determine whether those who fail to register a religious affiliation fare worse than those who register such?) But once again the placebo would become an unwelcome factor in one's reckoning. Maybe, as some studies have indeed suggested, religious people do better because they expect help from God. Maybe atheists do worse because they imagine themselves to be alone.

For the sake of discussion, however, let us grant that someday the value of petitionary prayer is somehow scientifically established, that Drs. Collip and Byrd and Krucoff turn out to have been unlikely pioneers. What shall we then think?

We shall still have no empirical proof that God answers prayer. How could a statistical regularity inform us about the mysterious Being who, at the burning bush, denied the possibility of being manipulated: "I will be what I will be"? Once it is shown, let us say, that, on average, those with a particular life-threatening illness have a 30 percent better chance of recovery if they are prayed for, surely we will not be so pedestrian as to imagine that God has finally been discovered by our scientific methods. That would make the Divinity a mechanism, a thing subject to human prediction and experimentation. We would instead declare the discovery of some new, natural, perhaps telepathic phenomenon. And we could add that our failure to fathom it makes it no different than photons or gravity.

This is the dilemma. If, on the one hand, the percentage of people who are prayed for and get well turns out to be close to the number predicted after we take into account normal rates of recovery as well as the data on spontaneous remissions and the placebo effect, then, as Laplace famously insisted to Napoleon regarding God, "Sire, I have no need of that hypothesis." If, on the other hand, that percentage is consistently higher than expected even after account has been taken of all other factors, we will, as the philosopher H. H. Price recognized, just have a new area for investigation: How is it that we direct subtle healing energies by thought alone?

I am reminded of those few investigators who have purported to show — I do not say have shown — that even plants respond favorably to prayer. Those researchers may be foolish (I do not know); but they are certainly not so foolish as to offer their statistical conclusions as proof of divine intervention. They think of themselves as scientists exploring a so-called parapsychological phenomenon. One need not be a theologian to observe that a God who chose not to halt the Holocaust is unlikely to assist oat seeds whenever asked.

The final paradox of petitionary prayer is that it can offer no solid evidence for either God's existence or God's activity. Although his theology is otherwise not mine, I agree with Martin Gardner: "It is impossible in principle to devise any sort of experiment, or make any kind of observation, that will be relevant to the hypothesis that asking God for something can make a difference."

This conclusion, that apparent answers to prayer cannot confirm religious convictions, seems exceedingly counterintuitive. But it in fact accords with common behavior. For in our prayers we do not usually ask for an incontrovertible manifestation of the Deity. We do not implore God to bring snow in July, or to run time backward, or to make $2 + 2 = 5$. It is instead our habit to ask for things we might otherwise obtain: recovery from pneumonia, return of a lost dog, strength for a new day. In short, we customarily expect God to act after a certain fashion consistent with the rest of our experience.

Intuitively we comprehend what Augustine argued — namely, that God does not work against what we call natural laws but through them. That is why we may trust the *Confessions* when it says that, after Augustine prayed, his toothache went away, but have some difficulty when the Venerable Bede informs us about the beheaded martyr who put his head back on and proceeded to sing. It is also why near the healing shrine at Lourdes there are mountains of crutches but not, as the wag observed, any wooden legs.

Providence cannot be espied in statistical aberrations. Rather does the invisible God typically work within the normal course of events. God follows the law of averages and so remains untraceable. This is why we can sincerely give thanks before meals without imagining that anything visibly extraordinary happened between farmer and grocer.

Philosophical theologians have debated how God can act without being noticed. Some have urged that God introduces infinitesimal changes beneath the surface of things, at the subatomic level. Others have speculated that, being outside space and time, the Supreme Being can make adjustments without destroying the chain of cause and effect. Origen offered that God foresaw our free acts and took them into account from the beginning of time. Whatever one makes of this murky issue that is beyond all of us, including the philosophical theologians, it remains obvious that God's activity is camouflaged. The divine labors are so covert that even those convinced they have seen prayers answered go through life without witnessing breaks in the normal causal nexus. As it says in Proverbs 25:2, "It is the glory of God to conceal things."

Perhaps the preceding reflections should trouble me more than they do. Maybe they should make me more cynical, or even move me to give up altogether asking God for this or for that. But they do not. I am sure that, on my deathbed, I shall, if not senile, still be asking God, among other things, to deliver my three children, Emily, Andrew, and John, from evil, to give to them the light of Christ, and to save them in this world and the world to come.

I wrote above that religious people are quite accustomed to doing and believing all sorts of things that pass understanding, and I include myself in this generalization. I do not try to squeeze all my religious thoughts and actions inside the borders of my mundane reason. There is just no fit. Nor, upon reflection, should we expect it to be otherwise.

As I ponder my place in this vast cosmos, my mind can move in at least four different directions. I can cast thought backward to the past, or forward to the future, or I can direct thought upward, to larger and larger things, or downward, to smaller and smaller things. In each case, the further my mind vectors away in any direction from my current location in time and space, the less it comprehends. As the past recedes or as I imagine the future, or as the world grows too large or too small for my five senses, my knowledge ebbs.

I know far more about tomorrow than I know about a year from now, and what will come to pass after I am dead and gone, or after the human race has ceased to be — who knows? The past, whether personal or universal, confronts us with the same circumstance. I can recall yesterday well enough, but my memories from when I was four years of age are so few that I can count them. In analogous fashion, we know a lot more about World War II than about the Crusades, and far more about the

Greeks than about the first Indo-Europeans. If we go back far enough, recall and history dissipate utterly. Eventually we have nothing more than the current speculations of cosmologists.

As with time, so with space: distance diminishes knowledge. The smaller something is, the harder it is to perceive it. We understand cars better than microbes, and microbes better than atoms, and atoms better than quarks. Indeed, the current, confused state of subatomic physics seems continually to confront us with things around which we may never comfortably wrap our thoughts. The same is also true of modern cosmology, which deals not with the minuscule but with the gargantuan: the unfathomably vast cosmos is largely terra incognito. We cannot see the universe as a whole, and anyone who follows the work of modern cosmologists knows that they, just like the subatomic physicists, are constantly being surprised and befuddled.

I like to think that I intuited our limitations when I was only a few years old. The first dream that I remember featured a plain giant pillar, a pillar whose top escaped my purview. Next to it was a tiny pillar, a pillar that I could just barely make out. The enormous contrast in size between the two objects — the dream contained nothing else — terrified me, so much so that more than forty years have not erased the nightmare. My uncomfortable place between the huge and the minute left me wondering where I was and who I was. I was lost between infinities.

The human mind, however precious, is an oasis of knowledge in a desert of ignorance that extends infinitely in all directions. And this is to speak only of the world of space and time. If there is a divine reality beyond or behind this one, our knowledge of it must be even more circumscribed.

I find it helpful in this connection to think about my dog Ralph, who is more German shepherd than anything else. Ralph knows that his food is kept in a large bag in the kitchen cabinet, and also that when I go to that cabinet with his dog bowl in hand, he is about to enjoy a meal. That is why he then barks with excitement. Ralph further knows that rubbing his large paws and whiskered nose against the cabinet in my presence communicates hunger, and that turning over his empty water bowl will get it filled immediately. Regarding his food and water, then, Ralph can think well enough.

There is, however, a fixed limit to his understanding. He does not know that bags of dog food come from a grocery store, a thing for which he has no concept. He does not know that a store has products because there are trucking lines. And he knows nothing about the agricultural operations or the manufacturing processes that result in bags of food. Such knowledge is too high for him; he cannot attain it.

These are things, moreover, that he can never understand. I could spend every waking hour trying to instruct him about the long chain of events that puts dog food in the kitchen cabinet. But it would all be in vain, for his mind is constricted. Beyond a knowledge of certain facts about the cabinet and his bowl, there is only fog. His mind runs out.

So too must it be with us. Some of us seem to imagine that because we understand much, we should be able to understand everything, and that science will continue pulling up the blinds, exposing to the light more and more of the dark room that is our ignorance. But this is a faith one need not be embarrassed to decline. Despite all our knowledge about ourselves and the universe we inhabit, much more is unknown than is known; our ignorance drowns our knowledge; and, just as Ralph's understanding soon enough meets what it cannot fathom, so too is it with us. The world is large, and our minds are small, so the latter cannot always contain the former. We cannot but expect there to be mysteries — permanent mysteries — on every side.

This is not to say, I must emphasize, that we should in any instance forsake critical reflection. The world is too full of evils bred of irrationality and nonsense for us to feel sanguine about neglecting our God-given minds or not thinking as hard as we can about everything, including the mysteries of our faith. We cannot neglect Aquinas as a bore or dismiss the Enlightenment as a passing inconvenience. Certainly we should never be quick to offer religious or unconventional explanations for something even if it initially leaves us nonplussed. Although the magicians still cannot tell us how Houdini made Jennie, his ten-thousand-pound elephant, disappear from the stage of the New York Hippodrome in 1918, we may be quite sure that nothing more than the magician's incomparable conjuring skill was involved. One guesses that someday somebody will figure out what he did.

Nonetheless, while we must pay due reverence to our marvelous critical capacities and use them to the full, good sense invites recognition of their limitations; and those of us who believe in a God who is more than the product of our psychological projections cannot live in accord with a promissory rationalism, with a belief that modern critical thinking will eventually tame everything. In some respects we remain forever like the dogs. So even if I do not understand exactly what I am doing — or rather, what God is doing — when I pray, I shall continue to pray. I shall continue to ask for the good things, for myself and for others. Petitioning the Deity is too much a part of the tradition I love and trust for me to pluck it out and throw it away. I moreover take some comfort in the knowledge that such petitioning is an almost inescapable activity of human beings. Surveys tell us that even most atheists pray to God for help once in a while. To pray is to be human. Why then should I deny my nature, especially when I believe that God fashioned it? I see no reason to disobey the invitation of the liturgist: "Let us pray."

The philosophical problems of petitionary prayer should, I think, concern us far less than the usual content of our prayers. Origen wrote,

> If we be given the spiritual gifts and receive illumination from God in the full possession of the things that are truly good, we shall not waste words over such an insignificant thing as a shadow. For all material and corporeal things, whatever they be, have no more value than a feeble and fleeting shadow. They can in no way stand comparison with the saving and holy gifts of the God of all. What comparison can there be between material wealth and wealth in all utterance and in all knowledge? And who but a madman would compare health of the flesh and bones with health of mind, strength of soul, and balanced reasoning?

Although many now feel uneasy with this sort of dualistic thinking, with its elevation of the spiritual and its denigration of the material, our religious faith cannot be entirely free of such. The God of the mystified Job and of the Crucified Man who had nowhere to lay his head is not, to state the blindingly obvious, in the business either of guaranteeing prosperity or of sparing us misfortune, so it is vain to ask for such. This is why our prayers should encompass more than normal daily cares, should ideally be not for money but for faith, not for success but for forgiveness, not for happiness but for charity. We should be as realistic and as noble as the pagan Marcus Aurelius, who advised his readers not to plead for immunity from hardship but instead to pray to be close to the gods when hardship comes, as it inevitably will.

No less problematic than the immature character of so much of our prayer is our failure to conduct ourselves as though prayer is, in the phrase of Clement of Alexandria and so many patristic authorities after him, "converse with God." Prayer, that is, is a sort of conversation, which means not monologue but dialogue. To identify prayer with petition, or even with thanksgiving, confession, petition, and praise, is to stay in the shallow end of the pool. We do not get to the deep end until we learn that prayer is much more than our own speech.

We are always talking to ourselves inside our own heads, and prayer is, in the first place, our natural response to the conviction that this incessant activity has an ever-present witness. As Simeon the Pious says in the Talmud, "The one who prays must see himself as if the Shekhinah were opposite him, as it says, 'I have set the Lord before me always'" (Ps 16:8). Now recognition of the divine presence, the presupposition of all silent prayer, cannot be without effect. This is partly what Calvin meant when he commented that we pray not so much for God's sake as for ours: prayer changes things because prayer changes us. One way this happens, as Donald Capps has urged, is that, as we pray, we anticipate God's view of the subject and so complete the dialogical circle: "It is within our human capacity to take the role of another, including God, and to see matters from God's own perspective."

I should like, however, to appropriate the analogy a bit differently.

Modeling prayer upon conversation implies that, in addition to speaking, we refrain from speaking. One-sided conversations are not usually very rewarding, and our experience in this matter holds equally for prayer: our chatter needs to cease. Our inner ears need to hear something other than our own inner tongues. This is why our tradition, in its wisdom, has developed multiple methods for creating stillness within, a stillness that might allow the ears of the soul to hear the divine whisper. Many Eastern monks have set out to do this by reciting again and again the Jesus Prayer, "Jesus Christ, Son of God, have mercy upon me, a sinner." Many Western monks have cultivated so-called passive or centering prayer through focus on a chosen, sacred word and a studied refusal to take up one's own thoughts. Whatever the means, the goal has been the same: to slow or stop the torrent of thoughts that ever floods our minds and keeps us from encountering what lies beyond, that being a place wherein speaking can defer to listening, wherein prayer can become not something that we do but something that we receive as we wait upon God in hope and faith. As C. S. Lewis wisely said, "The real labor is to remember to attend."

"Luminous meditation on God is the goal of prayer." These are the words of Isaac of Nineveh, who believed that our prayers should issue in stillness. The compassionate monk recognized that, in this life, such stillness will never become, except in a very few, absolute. This is why he counseled his fellow monks that, if they could not prevent their minds from wandering during prayer, they could at least see to it that their thoughts strayed in helpful directions. Isaac nonetheless exhorted his audience to look for a dark and silent closet within because he knew that such a place exists, and that God is waiting to meet us there.

Folklore has it that the best piano tuners are blind, and that this is so because inferior sight makes for superior hearing: the one sense comes to the rescue of the other. The myth is not uninformed. Neuroscientists have established that, when one sense is impaired, another may step in to help, and that, in particular, people's sense of hearing often becomes exceptional if they cannot see, especially when they have been blind from an early age. There is in this a lesson about our religious lives. For if there are physical senses, there are also spiritual senses; and just as hearing grows when sight diminishes, so too do our spiritual senses become more acute when the physical senses retreat.

The luminous dusk, the unspent, dark cloud of God's glory, lies beyond a door that is buried, in the words of Teresa of Ávila, "in the extreme interior, in some very deep place within." Although only God's grace can open the door, we can at least do our best to stand before the doorway. We do this by temporarily abandoning, during prayer and meditation, the world of the five senses, by declining to look at or listen to or think about the things around us. Darkness and stillness then become our collaborators, helping us to drag our attention away from this world of divertissement to the numinous world that holds the neglected fountain of divine light. The testimony of the saints is that this fountain, although hidden, can be found, or rather revealed, and that, when this happens, we are remade — and then sent back into the everyday, material world to do our mundane tasks with renewed life. Is this not the one great end to which we, on behalf of the whole world, should direct all our prayers?